THE ACCOUNTING SYSTEM

A Self-Study Preparation for Introductory Accounting

WILLIAM RULAND Ph

Professor of Accounting, Baruch C

City University of New Yor

SOUTH-WESTERN College Publishing

An International Thomson Publishing Company

I(T)P®

International Thomson Publishing
South-Western College Publishing is an ITP Company.
The ITP trademark is used under license.

Accounting Team Director: Richard Lindgren
Acquisitions Editor: David L. Shaut
Developmental Editor: David L. Shaut
Production Editor: Mike Busam
Designer: Michael H. Stratton
Marketing Manager: Matt Filimonov

ISBN: 0-538-88597-1
1 2 3 4 5 6 7 PN 2 1 0 9 8 7
Printed in the United States of America

THE ACCOUNTING SYSTEM
A Self-Study Preparation For Introductory Accounting

PREFACE

This booklet is a self-study introduction to the accounting system. It should be used before the first accounting course begins. Many students learn the accounting system more effectively at their own pace. It addition, pressures are often fewer before the busy semester begins.

The objectives of this self-study preparation are:

1. To help develop a solid understanding of the basic accounting system,

2. To permit students with no background in accounting to catch up to those with previous accounting exposure, and

3. To better ensure success in the first accounting course.

Students should practice the concepts rather than try to memorize the material. The recommended approach is to review the text and numerical examples. Then, work all exercises as a self-test. If you stumble on an exercise, review the earlier material and work the exercise again. Unhappy experiences in accounting courses often result from failure to understand the accounting system. By working through the booklet, you increase the likelihood of success in accounting and in your college business program.

FINANCIAL STATEMENTS

The accounting system provides for recording financial information, classifying this information, and developing financial statements. People in business use these financial statements in their work and in managing personal investments. In fact, many business managers rank financial statements among their most important tools. Financial statement users include investors when considering whether to buy, sell, or hold securities, lenders in evaluating loan requests, and suppliers when deciding whether to extend credit.

WHY USERS NEED SPECIFIC TRAINING

The first accounting course shows people in business how to work with financial statements. One might ask, "Why do statement users need to learn the accounting system? Can't everyone read?" The answers are that accountants use vocabulary and conventions that are not obvious without specific orientation. Successful athletes know the rules of their games. Similarly, successful professionals in business should know the accounting system.

THE ACCOUNTING SYSTEM
TABLE OF CONTENTS

CHAPTER 1

PAST PERFORMANCE AND CURRENT STATUS

(The Income Statement and Balance Sheet)

CHAPTER 1

PAST PERFORMANCE AND CURRENT STATUS
(The Income Statement and Balance Sheet)

All financial statements include income statements and balance sheets. A major objective of this short self-study course is to help users to become very comfortable with both documents. While working through this material, you will become very familiar with income statements, balance sheets, and their relationship to cash flow.

INCOME STATEMENTS

Income measures financial performance. It addresses the question of: "How well did we do?" Income is always measured over a prescribed period of time. This may be a month, a quarter, or a full year. Following is the income statement for Banana Rock, Incorporated, a store that sells records, tapes, and CDs:

Banana Rock Incorporated
Income for the Year ended December 31, 19x7

Sales Revenue		$240,000
Expenses		
Cost of Goods Sold	$90,000	
Other Expenses	80,000	170,000
Income		$70,000

Banana Rock's income statement begins with the name of the business and the period over which income is measured. In this case, income is for the full year ending December 31, 19x7. The statement shows three components common to all income statements. These are revenues, expenses, and income.

Revenues

Revenues are inflows to the business from providing services. Record shops and other retailers have sales revenue; advertising agencies have service revenues. Later we will see that revenues do not necessarily mean that cash is collected. For purposes of this course, think of revenues simply as providing services.

Expenses

Expenses reflect the use of services. Banana Rock's income statement shows three categories of expenses. One is the Cost of Goods Sold. As the title suggests, this is simply the cost of the goods that were sold during the period. Other expenses include rent, salaries, and electricity usage. Now, try the following exercises to be sure that you understand revenues and expenses.

Exercise 1-1: Revenues and Expenses. Talk-a-Lot, Incorporated, the local phone company is preparing its income statement. One item is the cost of preparing and mailing advertising brochures. This would include word processing, printing, and mailing. Is the cost of preparing and mailing advertising brochures an expense?

Exercise 1-2: Revenues and Expenses. Three of the following items relate to revenues and three relate to expenses for the Broken Buggy Shop, a gas station and repair business. Indicate R (for revenue) or E (for expense) as appropriate:

R E   Customers purchased oil and gas.
R E   Our service station manager paid the rent.
R E   We billed a customer $325 for car repairs.
R E   Broken Buggy let a local merchant sell flowers in the parking lot and billed her $125 for use of the space.
R E   Phone calls for the period cost $90.
R E   Property tax payments were $500.

Solutions:

Exercise 1-1. Yes, the cost of mailing is an expense. Word processing, printing, and mailing all entail the use of services.

Exercise 1-2. The first, third, and fourth items are revenues. Items two, five, and six are expenses. Remember that revenues mean providing services. When we charge customers who buy gas, who have cars repaired, or rent space from us, we have revenue. We use services when we rent space, make phone calls, and pay taxes (theoretically reflecting services provided by the government).

Income

Income is the difference between revenues and expenses. It measures financial performance. When revenues exceed expenses, the firm has income. Income is also called profit or earnings.

Exercise 1-3: Income. A portion of the Quick Start Company's income statement for the year shows:

Quick Start Company
Income for the Year ended December 31, 19x9

Sales Revenue		$2,100,000
Expenses		
Cost of Goods Sold	$1,400,000	
Rent Expense	200,000	
Salaries	200,000	1,800,000
Income		?

What is Quick Start's income?

Solution. The company's income is $300,000. This is the difference between revenues and expenses.

Usually, revenues exceed expenses resulting in a profit. When expenses exceed revenues, the difference is a loss.

Exercise 1-4: Income and Losses. A portion of the Dead End Company's income statement for the year shows:

Dead End Company
Income for the Year ended December 31, 19x9

Sales Revenue		$500,000
Expenses		
Cost of Goods Sold	$400,000	
Rent Expense	150,000	
Salaries	<u>200,000</u>	<u>750,000</u>
Income or loss		?

Which of the following reflects the Dead End Company's income or loss?

a. $250,000 income
b. $500,000 income
c. $250,000 loss

Solution. C. When expenses exceed revenues, income is negative. Dead End reports a loss for the year.

BALANCE SHEETS

Balance sheets report the situation at a particular point in time. While income statements show performance over a period of time, balance sheets give us a picture of the situation now. Balance sheets show assets, liabilities, and owners' equity.

Assets

Assets are items of value to the business. Examples include cash, inventories, investments, equipment, and buildings. Most of us are familiar with cash, investments, equipment, and buildings. Inventories are items purchased or manufactured for resale.

Specific income statement and balance sheet disclosures are referred to as accounts. For example, salary expense on the income statement is an account. Cash, Investments, and Equipment on the balance sheet are also examples of accounts.

Liabilities

These are amounts owed. They are the creditor's claims against the business. One example is loans payable. The account titles of many liabilities include the word "payable."

Exercise 1-5: Assets or Liabilities. Three of the following items are assets and three are liabilities. Indicate A (asset) or L (liability), as appropriate, for each item.

A L   Machinery
A L   Loan payable to a supplier
A L   Computer
A L   Loan payable to the bank
A L   Truck
A L   Loan payable to truck dealer

Exercise 1-6: Assets and Liabilities. The Frugal Company reports the following asset and liability accounts:

Frugal Company Assets and Liabilities
for the Year ended December 31, 19x7

Cash	$60,000
Bank Loan Payable	70,000
Inventory	30,000
Buildings	100,000
Equipment	200,000

Which of the following is the amount of the Dead End Company's total assets?

a. $390,000
b.   460,000
c.   500,000

Solutions

Exercise 1-5. Machinery, computers, and trucks are assets. The other items are liabilities. Remember that assets are items of value. Machinery, computers, and trucks certainly fall into this category. Liabilities are amounts that the business owes.

Exercise 1-6. A. All items except the bank loan payable are assets, items of value to the business. These four items total $390,000. The loan payable is a liability.

Owners' Equity

Owners' equity is the third major component of the balance sheet. It is the owners' interest in the business. Owners' equity represents the owners' claims against the business assets. Two components are contributed capital and retained earnings.

Contributed Capital

Contributed capital is the portion of owners' equity that owners contributed to the business. Owners of corporations hold shares of stock and are referred to as shareholders. For purposes of this course, assume that all contributed capital is capital stock.

Example: Capital Stock. The business began with a $10,000,000 investment from the owners. The owners later contributed an additional $15,000,000. The Capital Stock account balance is now $25,000,000.

Changes in Capital Stock

Beginning Capital Stock	$10,000,000
Additional Investment	15,000,000
Ending Capital Stock	$25,000,000

Retained Earnings

Retained earnings are the second main component of owners' equity. Retained earnings increase as corporations earn income. Declaring dividends reduces retained earnings. Dividends are distributions to the shareholders. Think of retained earnings as the earnings re-tained in the business (not declared as dividends).

Exercise 1-7: Retained Earnings. During the year, our company's income is $400,000 and dividends declared are $325,000. You can use the following table to find the increase in retained earnings.

Changes in Retained Earnings

Add: Income   _____

Less: Dividends Declared   _____

    Increase in Retained Earnings   _____

Which of the following choices shows the increase in retained earnings?

a. $75,000
b. 325,000
c. 400,000

Solution. A. The increase in retained earnings is $75,000. This is the current period's income less the dividends declared.

Retained Earnings account balances are cumulative. For profitable companies, the balances typically increase every year.

Example: Retained Earnings. The Pansy Company begins the year with $500,000 of retained earnings. Earnings for the year are $400,000. Pansy then declares dividends meaning that the company promises to distribute $200,000 of its earnings to owners. At the end of the year, retained earnings are $700,000 as follows.

Changes in Retained Earnings

Beginning Retained Earnings	$500,000
Add: Income	400,000
Less: Dividends Declared	-200,000
Ending Retained Earnings	$700,000

Note that dividends do not reduce income. Income measures financial performance. This is not influenced by dividends.

Exercise 1-8: Retained Earnings. The Puppy Corporation earns $50,000 in its first year, $60,000 in its second year, and $100,000 during the third year. Dividends declared are $20,000 each year.

Changes in Retained Earnings

Beginning Retained Earnings	$0
Add: Cumulative Income	_____
Less: Dividends Declared	_____
Ending Retained Earnings	_____

Which of the following represent retained earnings at the end of the third year?

a. $30,000
b.   40,000
c.   150,000

Solution. C. Cumulative income increases retained earnings. Declaring dividends reduces retained earnings.

Changes in Retained Earnings

Beginning Retained Earnings	$0
Add: Cumulative Income	210,000
Less: Dividends Declared	-60,000
Ending Retained Earnings	$150,000

We know that adding income to beginning retained earnings and subtracting dividends gives us ending retained earnings. Analysts can use this relationship to determine dividends or income given the other elements of retained earnings.

Exercise 1-9: Retained Earnings. The Fuzz Company begins the year with retained earnings of $150,000. During the year, the company earns $70,000. Ending retained earnings are $160,000. Use the following table to find the dividends declared.

Changes in Retained Earnings

Beginning Retained Earnings	$150,000
Add: Cumulative Income	_____
Less: Dividends Declared	_____
Ending Retained Earnings	$160,000

Select the choice to indicate the dividends declared by the Fuzz Company:

a. $35,000
b.   40,000
c.   60,000

Solution. C.   Retained earnings began at $150,000. Income then added $70,000, bringing the total to $220,000. Since the ending account balance is only $160,000, we know that dividends were $60,000.

Changes in Retained Earnings

Beginning Retained Earnings	$150,000
Add: Cumulative Income	70,000
Less: Dividends Declared	-60,000
Ending Retained Earnings	$160,0000

Exercise 1-10: Retained Earnings. The Tulip Garden Company begins the year with retained earnings of $200,000. During the year, the company reports income. It then declares dividends of $25,000. Ending retained earnings are $250,000..

Changes in Retained Earnings

Beginning Retained Earnings	$200,000
Add: Income	_____
Less: Dividends Declared	_____
Ending Retained Earnings	_____

Tulip Garden's income for the year is:

a. $25,000
b.   75,000
c.   250,000

Solution. B. Retained earnings increased from $200,000 to $250,000. The $25,000 in dividends declared, however, <u>reduces</u> retained earnings. Therefore, we know that income had to be $75,000.

Changes in Retained Earnings

Beginning Retained Earnings	$200,000
Add: Income	75,000
Less: Dividends Declared	- 25,000
Ending Retained Earnings	$250,0000

Go back to the Pansy Company example if you're not comfortable with these retained earnings exercises.

Exercise 1-11: Income, Dividends, and Retained Earnings. This exercise tests our ability to develop an income statement. Revenues, expenses, and dividends declared for Burger and Milk, Inc., a restaurant chain are as follows:

Burger and Milk, Inc.
Income for the Year ended December 31, 19x9

Sales Revenue	$900,000
Cost of Goods Sold	450,000
Rent Expense	140,000
Salaries	250,000
Dividends Declared	35,000

Income and the increase in retained earnings for 19x9 are:

a. $60,000 and $25,000
b. $60,000 and $0
c. $25,000 and $25,000

Solution. A. Income is $60,000. This is the revenue less the three expenses as shown on the following income statement:

Burger and Milk, Inc.
Income for the Year ended December 31, 19x9

Sales Revenue		$900,000
Cost of Goods Sold	$450,000	
Rent Expense	140,000	
Salaries	250,000	840,000
Income		$60,000

Retained earnings increase by $25,000 ($60,000 income less $35,000 dividends declared). Dividends declared reduce retained earnings, but do not reduce income. Dividends declared never show on the income statement.

Please go back to the beginning discussion of retained earnings and rework the previous exercises if you had trouble with this.

Exercise 1-12: Owners' Equity. Owners of the Sly Corporation invested $500,000 to begin the business and an additional $700,000 in later years. Sly Corporation earned $400,000 over the years and declared dividends of $250,000.

Which of the following are the correct balances in the Capital Stock and Retained Earnings accounts?

a. $500,000 and $400,000
b. $1,200,000 and $150,000
c. $1,200,000 and $400,000

Solution. B. Capital stock is the total amount invested in the business -- $500,000 initially and $700,000 in later years for a total of $1,200,000. Sly's retained earnings are $150,000, the cumulative earnings less dividends declared.

Changes in Capital Stock

Beginning	$500,000
Increases	700,000
Ending	$1,200,000

Changes in Retained Earnings

Cumulative Income	$400,000
Less: Cumulative Dividends Declared	-250,000
Ending Retained Earnings	$150,000

Go back to the contributed capital and retained earnings examples if you need help with this.

A Sample Balance Sheet

Earlier we looked at the income statement for Banana Rock, Incorporated, the record shop. Now we consider the corresponding balance sheet:

Balance Sheet for Banana Rock, Incorporated
At December 31, 19x7

Assets		Liabilities and Equity	
Cash	$75,000	Loan Payable	$20,000
Inventory	20,000	Capital Stock	120,000
Land	105,000	Retained Earnings	60,000
	$200,000		$200,000

Balance sheets and income statements always show the name of the business. This tells us that Banana Rock, Incorporated rather than some other entity holds the listed assets and is responsible for the liabilities. Similarly, income statements include only the income of the particular entity designated in the title of the statement. If owners have other sources of income or other assets, the other items would show on separate financial statements for these businesses.

In addition, balance sheets are always dated. This particular balance sheet shows account balances at the end of 19x7.

Exercise 1-13: Assets. Referring to Banana Rock's balance sheet, which of the following totals relate to items of value to the business?

a. $75,000
b.   95,000
c. 200,000

Solution. C. Cash, inventory, and land are all assets. These are the items of value to the business. The Loan Payable is a liability and Capital Stock is an owners' equity account.

Exercise 1-14: Owners' Equity. Select the correct amount of Banana Rock's owners' equity from the following choices:

a. $120,000
b. 180,000
c. 200,000

Solution. B. The owners' equity accounts are Capital Stock ($120,000) and Retained Earnings ($60,000). These accounts reflect the owners' interest in the business. The loan payable is a liability and is not part of owners' equity.

Go back to the descriptions of capital stock and retained earnings if you missed this one.

The Balance Sheet Equation

Assets, liabilities, and owners' equity are closely related. Reference to Banana Rock's balance sheet shows the following relationship:

Assets = Liabilities + Owners' Equity

The balance sheet equation relates assets and the claims against those assets. All balance sheets use this simple equation. Balance sheets serve at least two purposes. One is to show the various asset, liability, and owner's equity accounts. Another is to compare the claims to the company's assets.

Banana Rock's balance sheet shows two types of claims against the various assets. One is the bank loan, a liability. The other is owners' equity, the owners' interest. According to the balance sheet, assets are $200,000. Therefore, claims must also be $200,000. If the company discontinues business, the liabilities must be paid first. Claims by the owners always take a lower priority. Thus, if all assets are sold for only $150,000, lenders will receive $20,000 and the owners will receive the remaining $130,000.

An understanding of the balance sheet equation can be very useful in analysis. This is illustrated in the following example:

Example: The Balance Sheet. Suppose, that our copy of Banana Rock's annual report is damaged. We know the assets and liabilities, but can't read the owners' equity portion. If we know the assets ($200,000) and liabilities ($20,000), we can use the balance sheet equation to quickly calculate owners' equity.

Assets = Liabilities + Owners' Equity

$200,000 = $20,000 + Owners' Equity

Owners' Equity = $200,000 - $20,000 = $180,000

Exercise 1-15: Balance Sheet Relationships. We know that the Split Rock Corporation has liabilities of $60,000 and owners' equity equal to $90,000. Using the Assets = Liabilities + Owners' Equity relationship, what is the amount of the Split Rock Corporation's assets?

Solution. The assets are $150,000. We know that liabilities and owners' equity total $150,000. Since Assets = Liabilities + Owners' Equity, assets must also equal $150,000.

Exercise 1-16: Balance Sheet Relationships. Portions of the Princeton Company's balance sheet were damaged by a coffee spill. Luckily, we were able to read all items except those designated with question marks.

Balance Sheet for the Princeton Company
At December 31, 19x4

Assets		Liabilities and Equity	
Cash	$20,000	Bank Loan Payable	?
Inventory	200,000	Capital Stock	80,000
Land	90,000	Retained Earnings	120,000
	$310,000		?

Our challenge is to determine the Bank Loan Payable balance. A two-step approach is recommended. First, use the balance sheet equation to find the total liabilities and owners' equity. Then, calculate the liabilities. Which of the following is the correct choice for Princeton's Bank Loan Payable?

a. $80,000
b. 110,000
c. 200,000

Solution. B. Since Assets = Liabilities + Owners' Equity, we know the total liabilities and owners' equity must be the same as the assets, $310,000. Then, since owners' equity totals $200,000 (capital stock plus retained earnings), the $110,000 remaining balance must reflect the bank loan. The complete balance sheet is as follows:

Balance Sheet for the Princeton Company
At December 31, 19x4

Assets		Liabilities and Equity	
Cash	$20,000	Bank Loan Payable	$110,000
Inventory	200,000	Capital Stock	80,000
Land	90,000	Retained Earnings	120,000
	$310,000		$310,000

Exercise 1-17: Assets and Liabilities. All of the Fudge Company's balance sheet accounts except Retained Earnings are shown below:

Fudge Company Balance Sheet Items
At December 31, 19x7

Cash	$60,000
Bank Loan Payable	70,000
Inventory	30,000
Equipment	100,000
Capital Stock	150,000
Note Payable for Equipment	40,000
Buildings	200,000
Retained Earnings	?

Our interest is in knowing the Retained Earnings account balance. For this exercise we should first classify the accounts as assets, liabilities, or owners' equity. Then we can use the balance sheet equation to calculate the missing amounts.

Fudge's Retained Earnings account balance is:

a. $130,000
b.   390,000
c.   500,000

Solution. A. Retained earnings are $130,000. Assets (cash, inventory, equipment, and buildings) total $390,000. This means that liabilities and owners' equity must also be $390,000. Since the two payables total $110,000, owners' equity must be $280,000. Of this, $150,000 is capital stock. Thus, retained earnings must be $130,000. Fudge Company's complete balance sheet shows the following:

Fudge Company Balance Sheet
At December 31, 19x7

Assets		**Liabilities and Equity**	
Cash	$60,000	Bank Loan Payable	$70,000
Inventory	30,000	Note Payable	40,000
Equipment	100,000	Capital Stock	150,000
Buildings	200,000	Retained Earnings	130,000
	$390,000		$390,000

Exercise 1-18: Balance Sheet Relationships. Judy started a small corporation at the end of 19x7 by investing her own cash and borrowing $5,000 from friends. At this point, the business had assets consisting of $15,000 cash.

a. How much of her own money did Judy invest?
b. Prepare the balance sheet at the end of 19x7.
c. The balance sheet shows two sources of claims on the business assets. Which group of claims has first payment priority?

Balance Sheet for Judy's Corporation
At December 31, 19x7

Assets		Liabilities and Equity	
Cash	_____	Loans Payable	_____
		Capital Stock	_____
		Total	_____

Solutions:

a. Judy invested $10,000 of her own money. We know this because assets are $15,000, and liabilities are $5,000. Since Assets = Liabilities + Owners' Equity, owners' equity must be $10,000. Owners' equity, in this case, is composed solely of Judy's contributed capital because the business has not had an opportunity to generate retained earnings.

b. The balance sheet shows these relationships as follows:

Balance Sheet for Judy's Corporation
At December 31, 19x7

Assets		Liabilities and Equity	
Cash	$15,000	Loans Payable	$5,000
		Capital Stock	10,000
			$15,000

c. The two groups of claims are liabilities and owners' equity. Liabilities have the first payment priority. If the business dissolves, the owners may receive funds only after all liabilities are paid.

MONEY MEASUREMENT

You may have noticed that all the events identified for Banana Rock Incorporated were expressed in terms of dollars. This is a necessary condition for reporting items in the financial statements.

Unfortunately, some important events or conditions are difficult to express in dollars. Examples include the health of the company president and the satisfaction of customers. Consequently, these items cannot be recorded as transactions in the accounting system. This money measurement concept is one limitation of accounting. It means that the accounts do not reflect some items of interest to the company and to users of financial statements. Thus, analysts must go beyond accounting disclosures to truly understand a business. Accounting information, however, is an excellent starting point for business analysis.

Exercise 1-19: Identifying Transactions. The Watch-All-Night Corporation operates a chain of video tape rental stores. Recently, the company noticed that its inventory of tapes is not as extensive as that of its competitors. Watch-All's accountant does not include this potentially important information in the financial statements because:

a. Inventory does not show in the accounts.
b. The accounts are adjusted only when cash is received or paid.
c. The money measurement principle.

Solution. C. The money measurement principle prevents the accountant from recording information that is not easily expressed in dollar amounts. Watch-All-Night and other companies show their inventory at cost. We know that choice a is incorrect because inventory is an important balance sheet item. Choice b is also incorrect because we also know that many important accounting adjustments do not involve cash receipts or payments.

MAIN POINTS

Income
Income is a measure of financial performance.
It measures performance over a specified period.
The income statement includes revenues and expenses.
Revenues are providing services.
Expenses are the use of services.
If expenses exceed income, the business has a loss.
Dividends are distributions to shareholders.
Income is not reduced for dividends.

Balance Sheet Items

Assets are items of value to the business.
Liabilities are the creditor's claims, the amounts owed.
Owners' equity reflects the owners' claims, the owners' interest.
Contributed capital (capital stock) is the amount that owners contribute to the business.
Retained earnings increase with income and decrease with dividends declared.

Money Measurement Principle

The money measurement principle means that accounting statements show only those events and situations that can be expressed in terms of dollars. Other items such as the quality of products are not reflected directly in the accounts.

CHAPTER 2

RECORDING WHAT HAPPENED

(Transactions)

CHAPTER 2

RECORDING WHAT HAPPENED
(Transactions)

Accountants refer to events recorded in the accounting system as transactions. The first step in the accounting process is to analyze transactions.

ANALYZING TRANSACTIONS

Earlier we looked briefly at an income statement and balance sheet for Banana Rock, Incorporated, a store that sells records, tapes, and CDs. The following events occurred during Banana Rock's first year in business:

1.	Shareholders contribute cash to the business	$120,000
2.	The business pays cash for its inventory of records, tapes, and CDs	110,000
3.	Merchandise is sold to customers for cash	240,000
4.	The cost of goods sold to customers	90,000
5.	Borrowed from the bank	20,000
6.	Salary and other cash expenses	80,000
7.	Purchased land	105,000
8.	Declared and paid dividends to shareholders	10,000

As we work this chapter, we will learn to analyze transactions and prepare income statements and balance sheets. One central concept is that transactions lead to changes in either assets, liabilities, or owners' equity. In addition, we will discover that all transactions concern two or more accounts. We already know that:

Assets = Liabilities + Owners' Equity

Another simple, but important principle is:

All transactions have at least two sides

We'll see how these concepts work as we study Banana Rock's transactions.

1. **Shareholders Contribute Cash to the Business**. As a rule, businesses begin with cash contributions from the owners. When the business receives $120,000 from the owners, assets increase and owners' equity also increases. The asset is Cash and the owners' equity item is Capital Stock. This transaction satisfies the balance sheet equation, Assets = Liabilities + Owners' Equity. At this point, the balance sheet shows the asset and the owners' claim against the asset. In tabular form:

Description	Assets	Liabilities	Equity
Shareholders' contribute cash	120,000		120,000

2. **Acquire Inventory for Cash**. This transaction involves the $110,000 purchase of inventory for cash. Two assets are involved. One is cash. Cash payments reduce assets. The other side of the transaction is the increase in inventory. This part of the transaction increases assets. Total assets, however, do not change. Liabilities and owners' equity also do not change. When the company acquires inventory for cash, it replaces one asset with another asset.

Description	Assets	Liabilities	Equity
Acquire inventory for cash	110,000		
	-110,000		

Note that even though the business spends a great deal of cash, it does not record an expense. Expenses reflect the use of services. In this case, the expense comes later when the goods are sold.

3. **Cash Sales**. The third transaction concerns $240,000 of cash sales. The relevant accounts are Cash and Sales Revenue. Sales revenue increases income and income, in turn, increases retained earnings. Thus, Sales Revenue is an owners' equity account. We already know that receiving cash increases assets.

Description	Assets	Liabilities	Equity
Cash sales	240,000		240,000

Exercise 2-1: The Balance Sheet Equation. For each of the three transactions, we were careful to be sure that Assets = Liabilities + Owners' Equity. Consequently, this relationship must hold true for the total of the three transactions. The transactions considered to date are grouped in the following table. Sum the assets, liabilities, and owners' equity to be sure that the balance sheet balances.

Trans.	Description	Assets	Liabilities	Equity
1	Shareholders' contribute cash	$120,000		$120,000
2	Acquire inventory for cash	110,000		
		-110,000		
3	Cash sales	240,000		240,000
	Totals			

Solution. At this point, the business has $360,000 in total assets and $360,000 in total owners' equity. The balance sheet is in balance.

Trans.	Description	Assets	Liabilities	Equity
1	Shareholders' contribute cash	$120,000		$120,000
2	Acquire inventory for cash	110,000		
		-110,000		
3	Cash sales	240,000		240,000
	Totals	$360,000		$360,000

4. **The Cost of Goods Sold**. Sales revenue was recorded in the previous transaction. Now, we consider an offsetting factor. This is the expense pertaining to the $90,000 cost of goods sold. The cost of goods sold reduces income and owners' equity. Since much of the inventory was sold, the transaction recognizes the reduction in assets and the reduction in owners' equity.

Description	Assets	Liabilities	Equity
Cost of good sold	-90,000		-90,000

Exercise 2-2: The Bank Loan. You should have a pretty good idea of how to record transactions based on our work to this point. The next transaction is the $20,000 bank loan. This increases cash. It also increases another balance sheet category, an amount owed. Based on your understanding of asset and liability relationships, complete the following table:

Description	Assets	Liabilities	Equity
Borrowed from the bank			0

Solution. The bank loan increases cash and establishes a liability. Your entries should appear as follows:

Description	Assets	Liabilities	Equity
Borrowed from the bank	20,000	20,000	0

Expenses are the use of services. The cost of goods sold and other expenses reduce income. We can think of expenses as the opposite of revenues. Since revenues increase owners' equity, expenses reduce equity.

Exercise 2-3: Salary and Other Expenses. Complete the following table to reflect $80,000 in expenses and payments.

Description	Assets	Liabilities	Equity
Cash expenses			

Exercise 2-4: The Purchase of Land. This transaction is similar to the purchase of inventory (transaction two) in that one asset increases and another asset decreases. Complete the following table to show the purchase of land for $105,000.

Description	Assets	Liabilities	Equity
Acquire land for cash			

Solutions:

Exercise 2-3. Cash payments reduce assets. Expenses reduce income and owners' equity.

Description	Assets	Liabilities	Equity
Cash expenses	-80,000		-80,000

Exercise 2-4. The transaction showing the payment of cash in exchange for land is:

Description	Assets	Liabilities	Equity
Acquire land for cash	105,000		
	-105,000		

When businesses pay cash for assets, such as land, accountants record assets and the adjustment to cash. Buying land is not an expense.

Exercise 2-5: Dividends.   The last event is the declaration and payment of cash dividends amounting to $10,000. Dividends are distributions of profits to the owners. Earlier we learned that retained earnings increase with income. Retained earnings decrease when dividends are declared. Thus, one side of this transaction is concerned with the reduction of owners' equity to reflect dividends declared. We also know that cash, an asset, decreases when the dividends are paid. The transaction to reflect dividends declared and paid is:

Description	Assets	Liabilities	Equity
Cash dividends			

Solution. The declaration and payment of dividends reduce both assets and owners' equity as follows:

Description	Assets	Liabilities	Equity
Cash dividends	-10,000		-10,000

The following table summarizes progress to this point:

Trans.	Description	Assets	Liabilities	Equity
1	Shareholders' contribute cash	$120,000		$120,000
2	Acquire inventory for cash	110,000		
		-110,000		
3	Cash sales	240,000		240,000
4	Cost of good sold	-90,000		-90,000
5	Borrowed from the bank	20,000	$20,000	
6	Cash expenses	-80,000		-80,000
7	Acquire land for cash	105,000		
		-105,000		
8	Cash dividends	-10,000		-10,000
	Totals	$200,000	$20,000	$180,000

We see that the company's assets total $200,000. As expected, total liabilities and owners' equity also equal $200,000. Since we checked to be sure that each transaction balances, the totals must also balance.

At this point, we could prepare an income statement and balance sheet. However, we would need to reference the original events because our summary shows only whether the transactions increase or decrease assets, liabilities, or owners' equity. It does not show whether an adjustment to equity, for example, changes income or contributed capital.

We will now record the same eight events using a system that is more powerful than our simple row and column approach. While the transaction analysis is common to both approaches, the system to be presented provides for recording transactions in specific accounts.

T-ACCOUNTS

One deficiency of the simple row and column approach is that it doesn't show which specific accounts are associated with asset, liability and owners' equity items. We now learn how the system of T-accounts helps accountants summarize transactions and prepare financial statements. This system shows the information necessary to prepare the income statement and balance sheet. Once the data are recorded, it won't be necessary to refer to the original events.

We'll continue to work with the eight events considered previously. These are summarized as follows:

1. Shareholders contribute cash to the business $120,000
2. The business pays cash for its inventory
   of records, tapes, and CDs   110,000
3. Merchandise is sold to customers for cash   240,000
4. The cost of goods sold to customers   90,000
5. Borrowed from the bank   20,000
6. Salary and other cash expenses   80,000
7. Purchased land   105,000
8. Declared and paid dividends to shareholders   10,000

1. **Shareholders Contribute Cash.** We already know that this transaction increases cash and increases capital stock. In addition, we know that cash is an asset and that capital stock is an owners' equity item. This transaction is recorded in two T-accounts. T-accounts are named after their shape. They look like the letter T. One account is for Cash and the other is for Capital Stock.

Cash	Capital Stock
120,000 |	| 120,000

Notice that the entry for Cash shows on the left side of the T-account. Capital Stock shows on the right. This is consistent with three simple, but important rules.

Increases in assets go on the left

Increases in liabilities or owners' equity are opposite

Lefts = Rights

This last relationship means that entries on the left equal entries on the right.

You shouldn't need to memorize these simple rules. Practice with the exercises will make their application automatic.

2. **Acquire Inventory for Cash.** Previously, we determined that inventory increased while cash decreased for this transaction. Since increases in assets show on the left, we record the increase in inventory on the left-hand side. Then, since lefts equal rights, we need a right-side entry. Our right-side entry is to Cash as follows:

Cash		Capital Stock	
120,000			120,000
	110,000		

Inventory	
110,000	

Why does the adjustment to cash go on the right side? We know that increases in assets go on the left. Decreases are the opposite. Thus, this transaction illustrates a corollary to the basic rule for recording transactions. The basic rule is:

Increases in assets are on the left

The corollary is:

Decreases in assets are opposite

One helpful feature of recording items in accounts is that we can easily obtain the account balances. Examination of the cash account, for example, shows that the remaining amount is $10,000 ($120,000 offset by $110,000).

3. **Cash Sales.** Here, the company records $240,000 as sales revenue and the receipt of cash. Since cash is an asset, the entry to cash is on the left side. Earning revenue increases income (and retained earnings) and is shown on the opposite side, the right side.

Cash		Capital Stock		Sales Revenue	
120,000			120,000		**240,000**
	110,000				
240,000					

Inventory	
110,000	

Accountants work with right and left side balances all the time, and have assigned names to these entries.

Debits are left-side entries

Credits are right side entries

Thus, an entry to increase cash is called a debit. An entry to reduce assets is called a credit. Since lefts = rights,

Debits = Credits

Be careful to note that debits and credits don't mean good or bad. The only meaning is left or right.

Exercise 2-6: The Cost of Goods Sold. The cost of the goods sold to customers was given as $90,000. We know that the cost of goods sold is an expense, an income and owners' equity account. The other part of the transaction recognizes the reduction in inventory that was sold. Using your knowledge of left and right side entries, complete the list of T-accounts to reflect the cost of goods sold and adjustment to inventory.

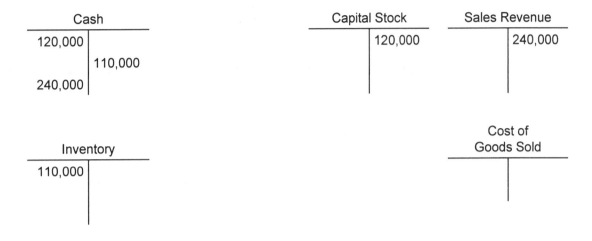

Solution. We debit the Cost of Goods Sold account because the expense reduces income (and owners' equity). Increases in owners' equity are credits; they go on the right. Decreases are the opposite.

Inventory is credited because this transaction reduces assets. Increases in assets go on the left. This decrease is on the opposite side. The completed accounts are as follows:

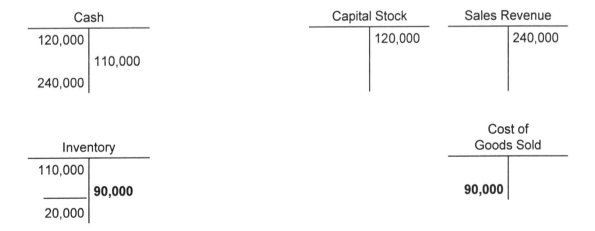

Banana Rock has drawn a horizontal line in the Inventory account and entered the $20,000 Inventory account balance. This means that remaining inventory is $20,000.

Exercise 2-7: The Bank Loan. We learned previously, that the $20,000 bank loan increases both assets and liabilities. Show the entries to record this transaction.

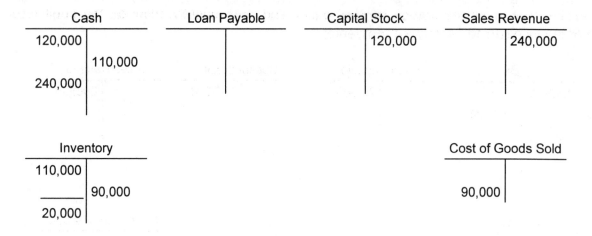

Cash		Loan Payable	Capital Stock	Sales Revenue
120,000				120,000	240,000
	110,000			
240,000				

Inventory			Cost of Goods Sold
110,000			
_____	90,000		90,000
20,000			

Solution. The increase in cash, of course, is a left-side entry, a debit. Since increases in liabilities and owners' equity items go on the right, we credit the Loan Payable account.

Cash		Loan Payable	Capital Stock	Sales Revenue
120,000		**20,000**	120,000	240,000
	110,000			
240,000				
20,000				

Inventory			Cost of Goods Sold
110,000			
_____	90,000		90,000
20,000			

Exercise 2-8: Expenses. Event number six reflects salary and other cash expenses of $80,000.

Remember that expenses reduce owners' equity and consequently show on the debit side. Record the expense and cash payment.

Cash		Loan Payable	Capital Stock	Sales Revenue
120,000			20,000	120,000	240,000
	110,000			
240,000				
20,000				

Inventory			Cost of Goods Sold
110,000			90,000
_____	90,000		
20,000			

Other Expenses

Solution. The following accounts reflect the reduction of owners' equity and cash for $80,00 in expenses. We debit Other Expenses to reflect the reduction in owners' equity. Cash is credited because this transaction also reduces assets.

Cash		Loan Payable	Capital Stock	Sales Revenue
120,000			20,000	120,000	240,000
	110,000			
240,000				
20,000				
	80,000			

Inventory			Cost of Goods Sold
110,000			90,000
_____	90,000		
20,000			

Other Expenses
80,000

Exercise 2-9: The Purchase of Land. Land was purchased for $105,000.

Since we previously recorded the inventory purchase, it should be straightforward to record the similar exchange of land for cash.

Cash		Loan Payable	Capital Stock	Sales Revenue
120,000	110,000	20,000	120,000	240,000
240,000				
20,000	80,000			

Inventory			Cost of Goods Sold
110,000	90,000		90,000
20,000			

Land			Other Expenses
			80,000

Solution. To record the purchase of land, we simply debit land and credit cash.

Cash		Loan Payable	Capital Stock	Sales Revenue
120,000	110,000	20,000	120,000	240,000
240,000				
20,000	80,000			
	105,000			

Inventory			Cost of Goods Sold
110,000	90,000		90,000
20,000			

Land			Other Expenses
105,000			80,000

Exercise 2-10: Dividends. Finally, the company declares and pays $10,000 in cash dividends. This entry reduces cash and reduces owners' equity. The specific owners' equity entry is a debit to Dividends Declared. Your challenge is to make this entry and then show the balance in the cash account.

Cash		Loan Payable	Capital Stock	Sales Revenue
120,000			20,000	120,000	240,000
	110,000			
240,000				
20,000				
	80,000			
	105,000			
____				

Inventory			Dividends Declared	Cost of Goods Sold
110,000				
____	90,000			90,000
20,000				

Land				Other Expenses
105,000				80,000

Solution. The complete set of accounts is shown below. Cash is credited in this transaction because payment reduces the asset. Dividends Declared is debited because this action reduces owners' equity.

Banana Rock's cash balance is $75,000, the net amount of the various debit and credit entries.

Cash		Loan Payable		Capital Stock		Sales Revenue	
120,000			20,000		120,000		240,000
	110,000						
240,000							
20,000							
	80,000						
	105,000						
_____	**10,000**						
75,000							

Inventory				Dividends Declared		Cost of Goods Sold	
110,000				**10,000**			
_____	90,000					90,000	
20,000							

Land						Other Expenses	
105,000						80,000	

When we recorded transactions the first time, we entered only the effect upon assets, liabilities, or owners' equity. The ending balances by account category are as follows:

Balance By Account Category

Assets	$200,000
Liabilities	$20,000
Owners' Equity	180,000
Total	$200,000

With the use of T-accounts, however, we can easily develop a more informative list of accounts. Summarizing account balances for the preceding list of T-accounts provides the following additional detail:

Account Balances

Assets		
Cash	$75,000	
Inventory	20,000	
Land	105,000	$200,000
Liabilities		$20,000
Owners' Equity		
Capital Stock	120,000-	
Sales Revenue	240,000	
Cost of Goods Sold	-90,000	
Other expenses	-80,000	
Dividends Declared	-10,000	180,000
Total		$200,000

JOURNAL ENTRIES

We know how to record transactions with T-accounts. A second approach uses journal entries. The debits and credits are the same with either method. Journal entries show all sides of the transaction in one place.   In contrast, when a large number of T-accounts are used, it's difficult to find all parts of the transaction. Thus, it is often helpful to record journal entries.

We just learned how to record eight transactions in T-account format. The first six transactions are as follows:

1.	Shareholders contribute cash to the business	$120,000
2.	The business pays cash for its inventory of records, tapes, and CDs	110,000
3.	Merchandise is sold to customers for cash	240,000
4.	The cost of goods sold to customers	90,000
5.	Borrowed from the bank	20,000
6.	Salary and other cash expenses	80,000

Now, let's consider the journal entry approach.

1. **Shareholders Contribute Cash to the Business**. We know that the debit is $120,000 to Cash and the credit is to Capital Stock. The journal entry format is as follows:

Cash	120,000	
Capital Stock		120,000

As indicated previously, this is just another way of considering the same transaction. Debits continue to go on the left and credits continue to go on the right. The corresponding numbers show in left and right columns. One advantage is that it is fairly easy to tell if debits don't equal credits. Another is that it's easy to see both sides of the transaction. Note that the debit comes first and that the credit is indented. Journal entries are always done this way. Debits are first; credits follow.

2. **Acquire Inventory for Cash**. When the company acquires inventory for cash, it debits inventory and credits cash for $110,000. In journal entry form.

Inventory	110,000	
Cash		110,000

_____

Exercise 2-11: Cash Sales. Try recording cash and sales revenue of $240,000.

_____	240,000	
_____		240,000

Solution: Your journal entry should appear as follows:

Cash	240,000	
Sales Revenue		240,000

Note that the debit showing the increase in cash is recorded first. Following this, and indented, the accountant shows the credit to increase owners' equity.

Exercise 2-12: Miscellaneous Journal Entries. Now record the following three events in journal format.

The cost of goods sold to customers	90,000
Borrowed from the bank	20,000
Salary and other cash expenses	80,000

_____	90,000	
_____		90,000
_____	20,000	
_____		20,000
_____	80,000	
_____		80,000

Solution. Your journal entries should show the following:

Cost of Goods Sold	90,000	
Inventory		90,000
Cash	20,000	
Loan Payable		20,000
Other Expenses	80,000	
Cash		80,000

Please refer to the corresponding T-accounts examined earlier for questions about any of these entries. The account titles, debits, and credits are identical for T-accounts and journal entries. Only the form of the entry differs.

MAIN POINTS

Transactions are events of interest in the accounting system.

The accounting process begins with identifying and recording transactions.

All transactions have at least two sides.

With respect to entries in the accounts:
    Increases in assets go on the left.
    Increases in other items are the opposite.
    Decreases in assets are also opposite.
    Lefts = Rights

Accountants call the left and right side entries debits and credits.
    Debits are left-side entries.
    Credits are right side-entries.
    Debits = Credits

Since individual transactions always balance, the total of all transactions must also balance.

Journal entries are an alternative way of showing the parts of a transaction.   The principle of
    debits and credits is the same with T-accounts and journal entries.

Exercise 2-13: Evaluating Events and Recording Transactions. Peter, Paul, and Marty just opened a color copy business. During the year, the following events occur:

1.	Shareholders contribute cash	$30,000
2.	The business buys paper and supplies	25,000
3.	Customers receive and pay for copies	180,000
4.	Paper and supplies used during the year	20,000
5.	Borrows from parents and friends	10,000
6.	Rent and salaries	120,000
7.	Declares and pays dividends	35,000

Your mission is to refer to the preceding example when necessary and record these seven transactions (1) in journal entries and (2) using T-accounts. Then, develop the list of account balances.

Journal Entries. Enter the appropriate accounts in the spaces indicated:

1. **Shareholders Contribute Cash**

   _____   30,000

   _____   30,000

2. **Acquires Paper and Supplies Inventory for Cash**

   _____   25,000

   _____   25,000

3. **Cash Sales (Customers Receive and Pay for Copies)**

   _____   180,000

   _____   180,000

4. **The Cost of Goods Sold (Paper and Supplies Used)**

   _____   20,000

   _____   20,000

5. **Loan Payable (the Business Borrows)**

_____   10,000

_____   10,000

6. **Rent and Salary Expenses**

_____   120,000

_____   120,000

7. **Dividends Declared and Paid**

_____   35,000

_____   35,000

T-Accounts. Now, record the same transactions in the following T-accounts:

Cash	Loan Payable	Capital Stock	Sales Revenue

Inventory		Dividends Declared	Cost of Goods Sold

Rent and Salary Expense

The List of Account Balances. Finally, show the account balances summarized from your T-accounts:

Account Balances

Assets
    Cash   _____
    Inventory   _____   _____

Liability   _____
Owners' Equity
    Capital Stock   _____
    Sales Revenue   _____
    Cost of Goods Sold _____
    Rent and Salary   _____
    Dividends Declared _____ _____
      Total   _____

Solutions:

T-Accounts

Shareholders Contribute Cash. Capital stock is an owners' equity account. The debit reflects the increase in the asset and the credit is to the increase in owners' equity as follows:

    Cash   30,000
        Capital Stock   30,000

2. **Acquire Supplies Inventory for Cash.** In this case, one asset increases and another asset decreases:

    Inventory   25,000
        Cash   25,000

3. **Cash Sales.** The debit is to cash and the credit is to Sales Revenue reflecting the increase in owners' equity.

    Cash   180,000
        Sales Revenue   180,000

4. **The Cost of Goods Sold**. The Cost of Goods Sold expense reduces equity. Inventory is also reduced because it is sold.

Cost of Goods Sold	20,000	
Inventory		20,000

5. **The Loan Payable**. With this transaction, both assets and liabilities increase as follows:

Cash	10,000	
Loan Payable		10,000

6. **Rent and Salary Expenses**. The expenses reduce owners' equity while the cash payment reduces assets.

Rent and Salary Expense	120,000	
Cash		120,000

7. **Dividends Declared**. Dividends Declared reduce owners' equity. The payment reduces assets.

Dividends Declared	35,000	
Cash		35,000

T-Accounts. Your T-Accounts should appear as follows:

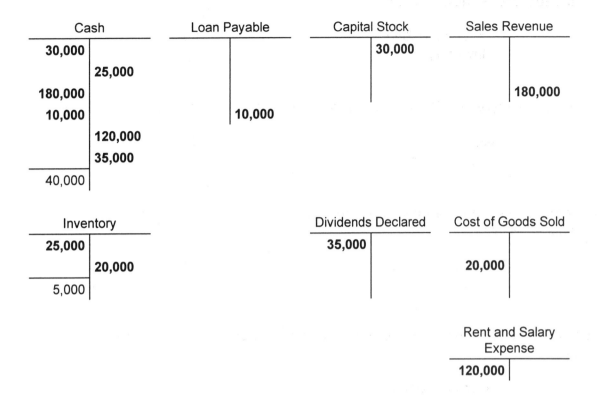

Cash		Loan Payable	Capital Stock	Sales Revenue
30,000			**30,000**	
	25,000			
180,000				**180,000**
10,000		**10,000**		
	120,000			
	35,000			
40,000				

Inventory		Dividends Declared	Cost of Goods Sold
25,000		**35,000**	
	20,000		**20,000**
5,000			

Rent and Salary Expense

120,000 |

The Account Balances

Based on the above T-accounts, the account balances are:

Account Balances

Assets		
Cash	$40,000	
Inventory	5,000	$45,000
Liability		$10,000
Owners' Equity		
Capital Stock	30,000	
Sales Revenue	180,000	
Cost of Goods Sold	-20,000	
Rent and Salary	-120,000	
Dividends Declared	-35,000	35,000
Total		$45,000

CHAPTER 3

PREPARING FOR NEXT YEAR

(Closing the Books)

CHAPTER 3

PREPARING FOR NEXT YEAR
(Closing the Books)

One function of accounting is to measure performance over a specified time period. This may be a week, a month, or an entire year. The measurement of annual income receives special emphasis.

After recording all transactions for the year, accountants close the books. Closing consists of transferring balances from temporary to permanent accounts. One objective is to calculate income and ending retained earnings. Another is to set revenue and expense account balances to zero at the end of the accounting period. Then, the business is ready to measure performance again next year.

PERMANENT ACCOUNTS

Accounts are classified as either permanent or temporary. Permanent accounts maintain their balances beyond the end of the accounting year. Nearly all asset and liability accounts are permanent. Capital Stock and Retained Earnings accounts are also in this category.

Example: Permanent Accounts: The Missile Corporation's Cash and Equipment account balances are $10,000 and $120,000 at the end of the business year. These accounts are called permanent because the account balances continue into the following year. Missile's books continue to show the same Cash and Equipment account balances on January 1 as on the previous December 31.

TEMPORARY ACCOUNTS

Revenue accounts, expense accounts, and Dividends Declared are referred to as temporary accounts. At the end of the business year, accountants always set the balances of temporary accounts to zero.

Example: Temporary Accounts: The Fishy Corporation's Sales Revenue and Cost of Goods Sold account balances are $100,000 and $70,000 respectively. These are temporary accounts and are closed at the end of the business year. Closing the accounts ensures that each year's income includes only revenues and expenses for that year. Fishy begins each January 1 with a clean slate. All revenue and expense accounts are zero.

THE CLOSING PROCESS

In the previous chapter we recorded transactions for Banana Rock, Incorporated. Now we will close the books and prepare the corporation's income statement and balance sheet. Steps in the closing process are:

1. Identify permanent and temporary accounts.
2. Close all revenue and expense accounts to Income Summary, a new account.
3. Close Income Summary to Retained Earnings.
4. Close Dividends Declared to Retained Earnings.

IDENTIFY PERMANENT AND TEMPORARY ACCOUNTS

From the previous chapter, after recording all transactions, the T-account balances for Banana Rock, Incorporated are:

Cash	Bank Loan Payable	Capital Stock	Sales Revenue
75,000	20,000	120,000	240,000

Inventory		Dividends Declared	Cost of Goods Sold
20,000		10,000	90,000

Land			Other Expenses
105,000			80,000

The first step in closing is to identify permanent and temporary accounts. All of Banana Rock's asset and liability accounts are permanent. Permanent accounts also include Capital Stock and Retained Earnings. The good news is that we ignore these accounts when closing. This leaves the following four temporary accounts to be closed:

> Sales Revenue
> Cost of Goods Sold
> Other Expenses
> Dividends Declared

Note that the net amount of the four temporary accounts is $60,000 as follows:

Account	Amount
Sales Revenue	$240,000
Cost of Goods Sold	-90,000
Other Expenses	-80,000
Dividends Declared	-10,000
Net	$60,000

When we finish, we'll see that retained earnings increase by $60,000.

CLOSE THE REVENUE AND EXPENSE ACCOUNTS

Our first step is to transfer the revenue and expense account balances to a new account called Income Summary. The entry to close Sales Revenue to Income Summary debits Sales Revenue and credits Income Summary as follows:

Cash	Bank Loan Payable	Capital Stock	Sales Revenue
75,000	20,000	120,000	240,000
			240,000 ___
			0

Inventory		Dividends Declared	Cost of Goods Sold
20,000		10,000	90,000

Land		Income Summary	Other Expenses
105,000		**240,000**	80,000

Now the $240,000 balance in Sales Revenue shows in the Income Summary account. Sales Revenue is closed. Next year, this account balance will begin to accumulate starting from a zero balance.

The process for closing the expense accounts uses the same rationale. Since expense accounts have left-side balances, these balances move to the left side of Income Summary. To close the Cost of Goods Sold account, we debit Income Summary and credit the Cost of Goods Sold as follows:

Cash	Bank Loan Payable	Capital Stock	Sales Revenue
75,000	20,000	120,000	0

Inventory		Dividends Declared	Cost of Goods Sold
20,000		10,000	90,000
			___ **90,000**
			0

Land		Income Summary	Other Expenses
105,000		240,000	80,000
		90,000	

Both Sales Revenue and the Cost of Goods Sold accounts now have zero balances. The previous balances, $240,000 and $90,000 were transferred to Income Summary.

Exercise 3-1: Closing Expense Accounts. The procedure for closing Other Expenses is the same as for closing the Cost of Goods Sold. Practice the closing process by closing Other Expenses. Then, take the new account balance for Income Summary.

Cash	Bank Loan Payable	Capital Stock	Sales Revenue
75,000	20,000	120,000	0

Inventory		Dividends Declared	Cost of Goods Sold
20,000		10,000	0

Land		Income Summary	Other Expenses
105,000		240,000	80,000
		90,000	

Solution. Your solution should show a debit to Income Summary and a credit to Other Expenses. The account balance for Other Expenses is now zero. Income Summary has a $70,000 balance.

Cash	Bank Loan Payable	Capital Stock	Sales Revenue
75,000	20,000	120,000	0

Inventory		Dividends Declared	Cost of Goods Sold
20,000		10,000	0

Land		Income Summary	Other Expenses
105,000		240,000	80,000
		90,000	_____ **80,000**
		80,000 _____	0
		70,000	

If you're not sure of this, go back to the section on closing the Cost of Goods sold.

The balance in Income Summary is the company's income. For purposes of this course, we can think of the Income Summary account as our income statement. It shows the same numbers as the income statement examined earlier.

Banana Rock Incorporated
Income for the Year ended December 31, 19x7

Sales Revenue		$240,000
Expenses		
Cost of Goods Sold	$90,000	
Other Expenses	80,000	170,000
Income		$70,000

CLOSE INCOME SUMMARY TO RETAINED EARNINGS

Now we close Income Summary to Retained Earnings, an owners' equity account. Debit Income Summary and credit Retained Earnings as follows.

Cash	Bank Loan Payable	Capital Stock	Sales Revenue
75,000	20,000	120,000	0

Inventory		Dividends Declared	Cost of Goods Sold
20,000		10,000	0

Land		Income Summary	Other Expenses
105,000		70,000	0
		70,000 ——	
		0	

		Retained Earnings	
		70,000	

CLOSE DIVIDENDS DECLARED TO RETAINED EARNINGS

At this point, Dividends Declared is the only remaining temporary account. We know that retained earnings increase with income and decrease with dividends declared. Thus, the final step is to close Dividends Declared to Retained Earnings.

Exercise 3-2: Closing Dividends Declared. Since Dividends Declared has a debit balance, the closing entry requires a credit to this account and a debit to Retained Earnings.   Show this entry in the following accounts:

Cash	Bank Loan Payable	Capital Stock	Sales Revenue
75,000	20,000	120,000	0

Inventory		Dividends Declared	Cost of Goods Sold
20,000		10,000	0

Land		Income Summary	Other Expenses
105,000		0	0

		Retained Earnings	
		70,000	

Solution. After debiting Retained Earnings and crediting Dividends Declared, the accounts appear as follows:

Cash	Bank Loan Payable	Capital Stock	Sales Revenue
75,000	20,000	120,000	0

Inventory		Dividends Declared	Cost of Goods Sold
20,000		10,000	0
		_____ **10,000**	
		0	

Land		Income Summary	Other Expenses
105,000		0	0

	Retained Earnings	
		70,000
	10,000	_____
		60,000

All accounts remaining with non-zero balances are permanent accounts. These permanent accounts comprise the balance sheet.

Finally, all temporary accounts are closed. We have developed both an income statement and the ending balance for retained earnings. Recall that we began by calculating the net amount of the four temporary accounts, $60,000. We now see that $60,000 is the addition to retained earnings. (Since the firm did not have beginning retained earnings, $60,000 is also the ending Retained Earnings account balance.) Thus, the balances in the temporary accounts do not disappear. They are merely transferred to Retained Earnings, a balance sheet account.

Why go through the income summary complication? We could have ignored this account and closed directly to Retained Earnings. Our procedure ensures that only income accounts are included in calculating income, the measure of financial performance. It also provides us with an income statement. One account that is never included in income summary is Dividends Declared. Dividends are distributions of earnings to owners. Financial performance is measured before providing for dividends. Following the steps outlined here helps to ensure against erroneously reducing income by the amount of dividends.

Test your understanding of the balance sheet with the following exercise.

Exercise 3-3: How The Numbers Get Onto The Balance Sheet. Our T-accounts correspond exactly with Banana Rock's balance sheet.

Balance Sheet for Banana Rock, Incorporated
At December 31, 19x7

Assets		**Liabilities and Equity**	
Cash	$75,000	Bank Loan Payable	$20,000
Inventory	20,000	Capital Stock	120,000
Land	105,000	Retained Earnings	60,000
	$200,000		$200,000

The balance sheet provides answers to a number of important questions. With respect to Banana Rock's balance sheet:

a.   What is the original cost of the businesses' assets?

b.   How much of the inventory remains?

c.   How much does Banana Rock owe at the end of the year?

d.   How much did the business owners invest since the business began?

e.   What is the owners' claim on the business assets?

Solutions.

a.   Banana Rock's assets originally cost $200,000, the amount shown for total assets.

b.   The cost of ending inventory is shown as $20,000.

c.   Liabilities are $20,000, the loan payable.

d.   Capital stock is $120,000. This is the amount invested by the owners.

e.   Owners' equity is the owners' claim. The amount is $180,000. It consists of capital stock and retained earnings.

KEY CONCEPTS IN MEASUREMENT

Now that we understand the basics of the accounting system, we should consider key concepts in income measurement. Important principles that govern the measurement of income statement and balance sheet items include the cost principle, conservatism, and the going concern assumption.

Cost Principle

Most assets including inventories, buildings, and equipment are recorded on the books at their historical cost. Accountants do not usually attempt to show these items at market values. One reason is that accounting information may be more reliable to users if based on easily verifiable information that is not subject to disagreement. Costs and values often differ. While people may agree on the costs of assets, they are less likely to agree on market values. This means that persons who are interested in the current values of assets must look to sources other than financial statements for this information.

Principle of Conservatism

Accountants are trained to take a conservative approach when recording assets and liabilities. Therefore, when in doubt, accountants record assets at lower amounts and record liabilities at higher amounts. For example, if the ability to collect receivables becomes doubtful, accountants generally reduce the amounts shown on the books for these assets. Of course, they still attempt to collect the amounts due. Similarly, when accountants expect future obligations such as payments of health benefits to retired employees, they record liabilities for these amounts. This is done even though future changes in health plans may reduce benefit payments to lower amounts.

Going Concern Assumption

Accountants generally assume that businesses will continue to operate as going concerns. Therefore, equipment and other assets show on the books at historical cost or adjusted historical cost. In rare situations when accountants question the going concern assumption for a particular business, they are trained to take a conservative approach. This means reducing assets to expected liquidation prices (for going out of business sales). When accountants make exceptions to the going concern assumption and reduce asset carrying values to expected selling prices, they are applying the principle of conservatism.

Exercise 3-4: Measurement Concepts. The Sell-A-Lot Corporation just learned that the Too-Low Corporation, a customer, has run short of cash and has declared bankruptcy. Too-Low's prices were so low that the company couldn't earn a profit. Sell-A-Lot is concerned that it will not collect $500,000 payable by the Too-Low Corporation. While this will not threaten Sell-A-Lot's ability to remain in business, it will reduce the company's cash flow. In accord with generally accepted accounting principles, the company reduces the receivable to a lower amount. This is an application of:

a. The concept that revenue is recorded in the accounts when services are provided
b. The principle of conservatism
c. The going concern assumption

Solution. B. The principle of conservatism suggests writing the receivables down to a lower amount. This principle holds that when in doubt, assets should be shown at lower amounts and liabilities should be shown at higher amounts.

While revenue is recorded in the accounts when services are provided, this is not the main issue here. The issue presented in this case relates to the adjustment of assets. C is not the most appropriate choice since Sell-A-Lot's ability to continue as a going concern has not been questioned. Therefore, B seems to be the best choice.

MAIN POINTS

The closing process consists of four steps. These are:

1. Identify permanent and temporary accounts.
2. Close all revenue and expense accounts to Income Summary, a new account.
3. Close Income Summary to Retained Earnings.
4. Close Dividends Declared to Retained Earnings.

Closing accomplishes several purposes. It sets all temporary account balances to zero in preparation for the next accounting period, it calculates income, and it develops a balance sheet. The Income Summary account serves as an income statement. Use of a separate Income Summary account ensures that dividends are not closed to income.

We also learned about the cost principle, principle of conservatism, and the going concern assumption. The cost principle holds that assets are generally recorded at their historic cost. Usually, this is the purchase price. The principle of conservatism encourages accountants not to overstate the recorded amounts of assets and equity. Consistent with the going concern assumption, accountants generally assume that businesses will continue to operate as going concerns and consequently do not record assets at expected liquidation amounts.

Exercise 3-5: Closing Revenue and Expense Accounts. After recording all transactions for 19x5, the WinSome Company's books show various permanent and temporary accounts. Beginning with the following account balances close all revenue and expense accounts to income summary.

Cash	Bank Loan Payable	Capital Stock	Sales Revenue
25,000	10,000	40,000	300,000

Inventory		Retained Earnings	Cost of Goods Sold
10,000		9,000	170,000

Investments		Dividends Declared	Other Expenses
50,000		4,000	100,000

Income Summary

Solution.   The three income statement accounts are Sales Revenue, the Cost of Goods Sold, and Other Expenses.   Since Sales Revenue has a right-side balance, the $300,000 amount moves to the right side of Income Summary. The Cost of Goods Sold and Other Expenses both have debit balances and these move to the debit side of income summary.   Income summary is the net amount, $30,000.   This is basically the company's income statement.

Cash	Bank Loan Payable	Capital Stock	Sales Revenue	
25,000	10,000	40,000	**300,000**	300,000
				0

Inventory		Retained Earnings	Cost of Goods Sold	
10,000		9,000	170,000	**170,000**
			0	

Investments		Dividends Declared	Other Expenses	
50,000		4,000	100,000	**100,000**
			0	

Income Summary	
	300,000
170,000	
100,000	
	30,000

If you had trouble with this, it should help to work the main example in the chapter and try this exercise again.

Exercise 3-6: Closing Income Summary and Dividends Declared. In the previous exercise, we closed the WinSome Company's revenue and expense accounts. Now, our challenges are to close Income Summary and Dividends Declared to Retained earnings and to prepare a balance sheet.

Close the Income Summary and Dividends Declared accounts to Retained Earnings and complete the following balance sheet.

Balance Sheet for Winsome Company
At December 31, 19x5

Assets		Liabilities and Equity	
Cash	_____	Bank Loan Payable	_____
Inventory	_____	Capital Stock	_____
Investments	_____	Retained Earnings	_____
	_____		_____

Cash	Bank Loan Payable	Capital Stock	Sales Revenue
25,000	10,000	40,000	0

Inventory		Retained Earnings	Cost of Goods Sold
10,000		9,000	0

Investments		Dividends Declared	Other Expenses
50,000		4,000	0

	Income Summary	
	30,000	

Solution. The final two steps are to close Income Summary and Dividends Declared to Retained Earnings. First, Income Summary's credit balance transfers to Retained Earnings. Then, the $4,000 Dividends Declared balance transfers to the debit side of Retained Earnings. This results in the following balance sheet:

Balance Sheet for Winsome Company
At December 31, 19x5

Assets		Liabilities and Equity	
Cash	$25,000	Bank Loan Payable	$10,000
Inventory	10,000	Capital Stock	40,000
Investments	50,000	Retained Earnings	35,000
	$85,000		$85,000

Winsome's T-accounts are as follows:

Cash			Bank Loan Payable		Capital Stock		Sales Revenue	
25,000				10,000		40,000		0

Inventory		Retained Earnings		Cost of Goods Sold	
10,000			9,000	0	
			30,000		
		4,000			
			35,000		

Investments		Dividends Declared		Other Expenses	
50,000		4,000		0	
			4,000		
		0			

Income Summary	
	30,000
30,000	
	0

Notice that the Winsome Company began the year with a $9,000 balance in retained earnings. When we add the current year's income and subtract dividends declared, retained earnings increase by $26,000. Thus, the ending retained earnings balance is $35,000.

Exercise 3-7: Comprehensive Transaction Analysis and Closing the Books. The Red Flag Corporation, a management consulting firm, experienced the following events during 19x2:

1.	Revenues	$750,000
2.	Salary expense	400,000
3.	Interest revenue received from investments	40,000
4.	Other expenses	90,000
5.	Declared dividends to shareholders	85,000
6.	Paid dividends	80,000

Beginning balances are shown in the following accounts. Record the transactions, close the books, and calculate retained earnings after all closing entries. (Hint: Dividends declared increase dividends payable, a liability. This liability is later reduced when the company actually pays the dividends.)

Cash
40,000

Dividends Payable
80,000 | 85,000
       5700
            5000

Capital Stock
| 70,000

Revenues
| 750000

Investments
460,000

Retained Earnings
85000 | 430,000
        300 000
        5000
        645000

Salary Expense
400 000

Dividends Declared
85000 |

Other Expenses
90,000 |

Income Summary
400000 | 750 000
90000 | 40000
300 000 |
        | 790

Interest Revenue
| 40,000

Solution. After recording the six transactions, the books appear as shown below.

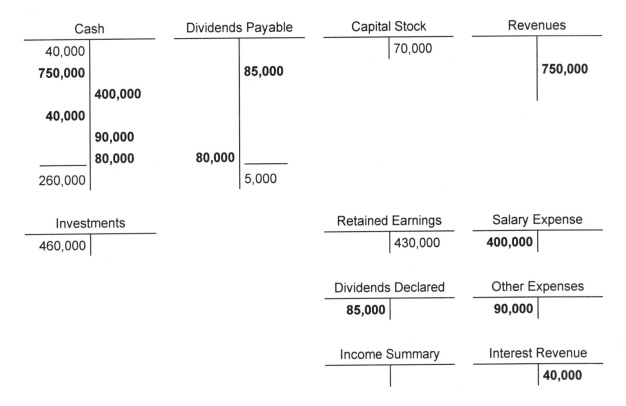

These transactions are very similar to the ones that you previously recorded. Please review the earlier material if you have questions. The only new transactions concern dividends. When the company declares dividends, it announces a promise to pay, a liability. Usually, any unpaid dividends are paid next year. Thus, the declaration of dividends is reported as:

Dividends Declared	85,000	
Dividends Payable		85,000

The current year payment then removes the liability as follows:

Dividends Payable	80,000	
Cash		80,000

Red Flag's entries to close are:

Cash		Dividends Payable		Capital Stock		Revenues	
260,000			5,000		70,000		750,000
						750,000	
							0

Investments				Retained Earnings		Salary Expense	
460,000					430,000	400,000	
					300,000		**400,000**
				85,000		0	
					645,000		

				Dividends Declared		Other Expenses	
				85,000		90,000	
					85,000		**90,000**
				0		0	

				Income Summary		Interest Revenue	
					750,000		40,000
				400,000		**40,000**	
				90,000			0
					40,000		
					300,000		
				300,000			
					0		

Following the usual procedure, Red Flag first closed the revenue and expense accounts to Income Summary. Income is $300,000 as shown in the subtotal for Income Summary. Then, Income Summary and Dividends Declared were closed to Retained Earnings.

Red Flag has closed all temporary accounts. The remaining accounts are permanent meaning that they show on the balance sheet. This balance sheet appears as follows:

Red Flag Corporation Balance Sheet
At December 31, 19x2

Assets		Liabilities and Equity	
Cash	$260,000	Dividends Payable	$5,000
Investments	460,000	Capital Stock	70,000
	$720,000	Retained Earnings	645,000
			$720,000

Red Flag's balance sheet shows cash and other items of value totaling $720,000. Then, liabilities and owners' equity must also equal $720,000. This is necessary because Assets = Liabilities + Equity is a necessary condition for any balance sheet. Of the three liability and equity items, dividends payable is the single liability.

Note that revenues, expenses, and dividends declared do not appear on balance sheets. These temporary accounts are always closed to retained earnings. It is possible to skip the income summary account and close all temporary accounts directly to retained earnings. The problem is that it's easy to become confused with respect to which items are included in income. We know that dividends declared reduce retained earnings directly; they never reduce income. Thus, income is $300,000 while the overall increase in retained earnings is only $215,000 due to declaring dividends.

CHAPTER 4

INCOME ISN'T ALWAYS CASH

(Accrual Basis Accounting)

CHAPTER 4

INCOME ISN'T ALWAYS CASH
(Accrual Basis Accounting)

This chapter and those that follow continue to develop key concepts in the accounting system. The exercises included in each of the chapters are presented in two sections. Each chapter's main body includes exercises which emphasize operation of the accounting system. Most people who work with accounting information, however, function as analysts. Analysts often examine income statements, balance sheets, and other accounting information and estimate the underlying transactions. The exercises in the appendices emphasize analysis techniques. They also provide preparation for cash flow analysis, an important topic in your accounting course. Try to work them, in addition to the exercises in the main part of the chapter, unless your instructor designates them as optional.

For most transactions examined to this point, we recorded revenues and expenses when cash was received or paid. In practice, however, services may be provided or received at one point in time with cash collections occurring earlier or later. Accrual basis accounting refers to differences in the timing of income statement items and cash receipts or payments. In other words, revenue and expense recognition does not always correspond to the timing of cash receipts and payments.

This chapter illustrates common accrual basis accounting transactions. A main purpose is to add to our understanding of changes in several key income statement and balance sheet accounts.

ACCOUNTS RECEIVABLE

Businesses usually ship goods to commercial customers before receiving payment. Customers, for example, might be given 30 days from the date of delivery to pay for goods. One reason is that buyers and sellers don't actually meet when goods are shipped by truck or rail.

Example: Goods Sold On Account. Might Industries ships goods valued at $50,000 to Fright Industries with payment due in 30 days. Might's journal entry at the time of shipment is:

Accounts Receivable	50,000	
Sales Revenue		50,000

Accounts receivable are assets. They are very valuable assets because in most cases, receivables quickly become cash. When payment is received, the seller's entry is:

Cash	50,000	
Accounts Receivable		50,000

In T-account form, the initial entry to record the receivable is:

Accounts Receivable	Cash	Sales Revenue
50,000		50,000

On receipt of the cash, the entry is:

Accounts Receivable	Cash	Sales Revenue
50,000		50,000
50,000	50,000	
0		

Since cash receipts tend to follow sales, the balance sheets of businesses that sell on account always show accounts receivable. An example follows:

Example: Sales on Account. The Cat Corporation sells goods on account during the year for $50,000. Collections this year are $40,000. Next year, sales on account are $55,000 and collections are $48,000. For the first year, Cat's T-accounts show:

Accounts Receivable	Cash	Sales Revenue
50,000		50,000
40,000	40,000	
10,000		

Year 2's entries are:

Accounts Receivable	Cash	Sales Revenue
10,000		
55,000		55,000
48,000	48,000	
17,000		

Note the relationship between the Accounts Receivable balance, cash received, and sales revenue. In the first year, Accounts Receivable increased by $10,000. This is the difference between revenue and cash received. Similarly, in the second year, the account balance increased by $7,000 (from $10,000 to $17,000) because Year 2 sales revenue also exceeded the cash collected that year.

Corporations and analysts are interested in accounts receivable for several reasons. One reason is that receivables are valuable assets. A second is that increases in receivables represent revenue not yet collected.

Exercise 4-1: Accounts Receivable. Increases in accounts receivable represent current year's sales not yet collected. Which is true for decreases in accounts receivable?

a. Decreases in receivables usually mean that cash collections exceed current period sales.

b. Decreases in receivables usually mean that cash collections are less than current period sales.

c. Changes in receivables are hard to interpret.

Solution: A. When accounts receivable decrease, the business has probably collected more cash than the current year sales. Choice b is incorrect because it's the opposite.

For example, assume that the Snaffle Corporation, a manufacturer of iced tea products, begins the year with $100,000 in inventory ($ in thousands). During the year, Snaffle sells beverages on account for $700,000 and collects $740,000 from customers. Since collections exceed sales by $40,000, receivables decrease by $40,000 as shown in the following T-accounts:

Accounts Receivable		Cash		Sales Revenue	
100,000					700,000
700,000					
	740,000	740,000			
60,000					

Exercise 4-2: Sales on Account. This exercise provides practice working with the Accounts Receivable, Cash, and Sales accounts.

During Year 1, the Frosty Company sells goods on account for $80,000. Collections are $60,000. Sales on account in Year 2 are $90,000 and collections are $85,000. Show the T-account entries and calculate the ending balance in Accounts Receivable.

Year 1:

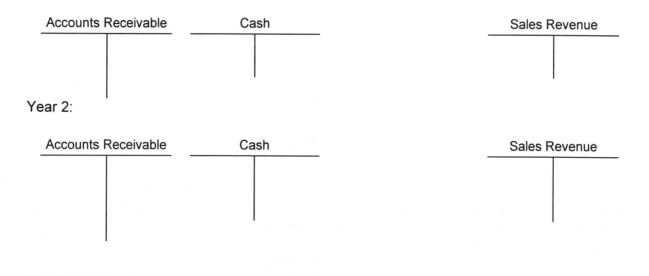

Year 2:

Solution: Each year, accounts receivable increase with sales and decrease with cash collections. The completed accounts for Year 1 are as follows:

Year 1:

The first entry shows $80,000 sales revenue and the increase in accounts receivable. Then, accounts receivable is reduced as the company collects cash.

For Year 2:

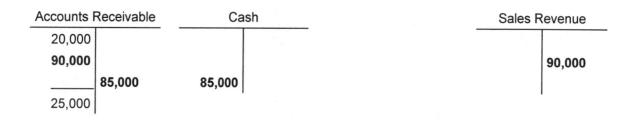

ACCOUNTS PAYABLE

When one party sells goods on account, the other party pays on account. Sellers record Accounts Receivable and buyers record Accounts Payable. Earlier we examined the sale of goods on account by Might Industries. Now, we consider Fright Industries, the buyer:

Example: Purchases On Account. Might Industries ships goods valued at $50,000 to Fright Industries with payment due in 30 days. Fright's journal entries to record the receipt of goods and the later payment are:

Inventory	50,000	
Accounts Payable		50,000
Accounts Payable	50,000	
Cash		50,000

In T-account form:

Cash		Inventory		Accounts Payable	
		50,000			**50,000**
50,000				**50,000**	
					0

Note that the buyer's entries are pretty much a mirror image of the entries made by the seller. One party shows receivables and the other shows payables. Similarly, one receives cash and the other pays cash.

Exercise 4-3: Purchases on Account. This exercise illustrates relationships between the Cash, Inventory, and Accounts Payable accounts. It also illustrates that the amount paid for inventory is rarely the same as the amount of purchases on account.

The Toast Company buys goods on account during Year 1 for $80,000. Payments this year are $60,000. During Year 2, purchases are $90,000 and payments are $85,000. The assignment is to record these transactions and calculate ending balances.

Year 1:

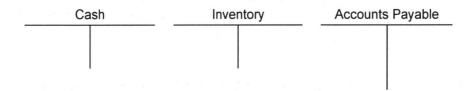

Year 2:

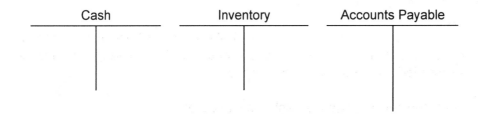

Solution. Accounts payable increase with purchases and decrease as payments are made. T-accounts for each of the two years show that accounts payable increase to $20,000 at the end of the first year and by an additional $5,000 at the end of Year 2.

Year 1:

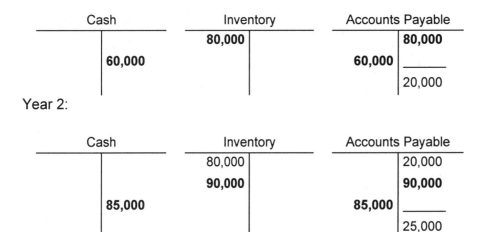

Year 2:

The Toast Company should also have sold much of its inventory. We ignore reductions in inventory for this problem since the purpose is to focus on purchases and accounts payable.

OTHER EXPENSES PAYABLE

Other common expense accruals relate to wages, utility expenses, and interest.

Wages Payable

Wages payable are amounts due to employees at the end of the accounting period. Typically, employees work for one or more weeks before they are paid. Consequently, an employee who starts work early in December may only receive one paycheck for the month with the second check due in early January. The employer, however, should record wage expense for the services used for the full month.

Example: Wages Payable. Andy Harper begins work at the Whiz Company on December 1, 19x4. His $3,000 per month salary is payable every two weeks. Due to the time necessary to process paperwork, Whiz writes Andy's first paycheck amounting to $900 on December 20. The next check is scheduled for early January, 19x5.

The company used Andy's services for the full month and should record wage expense of $3,000. Since only $900 is paid during 19x4, the remainder of the $3,000 expense is payable next year. This amount is recorded as Wage Payable, a liability.

Entries to record the expense, the liability, and the cash payment are:

Wage Expense	3,000	
Wages Payable		3,000
Wages Payable	900	
Cash		900

This leaves an ending liability of $2,100 as follows:

Cash		Wages Payable		Wage Expense	
			3,000	**3,000**	
	900	**900**			
			2,100		

Compound Entries

In the Andy Harper example, we recorded wage expense and the payment as two separate entries. An alternative approach is to use a compound entry. We know that all transactions must have at least two parts to maintain the balance sheet equality. Compound entries have more than two parts.

Example: The Compound Entry. Andy Harper's salary is $3,000 per month payable every two weeks. During the first year of employment, however, he actually received only $900 with the balance payable early next year. We learned to make the following entries:

Wage Expense	3,000	
Wages Payable		3,000
Wages Payable	900	
Cash		900

A compound entry accomplishes the same purpose with a little less writing:

Wage Expense	3,000	
Cash		900
Wages Payable		2,100

The convention, as with any journal entry, is to record the debit first. Credits are indented. If there is more than one debit or credit account, first record all debits; then all credits. It's easier to record one compound entry than two single entries. Another advantage, in this case, is that the compound entry clearly highlights the $2,100 increase in Wages Payable.

Exercise 4-4: Compound Entries. During the year, the Frosty Company purchases inventory on account for $120,000 and pays $100,000 to suppliers. Fill in the account titles for Frosty's transactions. Then, show these transactions as one compound entry

With two simple entries, to record purchases:

_____	120,000	
_____		120,000

To record payments:

_____	100,000	
_____		100,000

As a compound entry:

_____	120,000	
_____		100,000
_____		20,000

Solution

With two simple entries:

Inventory	120,000	
Accounts Payable		120,000
Accounts Payable	100,000	
Cash		100,000

Frosty debits inventory to reflect the increase in assets. The $120,000 credit to Accounts Payable, a liability, reflects the promise to pay for the goods. Frosty then reduces the liability when the company pays suppliers. Since accounts payable increase by $20,000 ($120,000 owed for purchases less $100,000 paid), the entries can be summarized in compound form as follows:

Inventory	120,000	
Cash		100,000
Accounts Payable		20,000

Note that the debit always comes first. Then, both credits follow. The purpose of this exercise is to illustrate compound entries. Since the company bought and paid for inventory at different times, it would use the two-entry approach in practice.

Utility Expenses Payable

Many expenses including those relating to electricity, long-distance telephone charges, and other expenses are routinely paid on account. Businesses (and individuals) typically delay payment until the bill is due.

Exercise 4-5: Expenses Payable. This is the first year of business for the Little Bird Company.   During the year, Little Bird received telephone bills amounting to $25,000. The last bill was for $1,500. It was received on December 23 and is payable in January.   Consequently, only $23,500 of the $25,000 in expenses were paid during the year. Show a simple entry to record the phone bills received for the year and a second simple entry to record the payments. Then, show the same transactions using a compound entry.

The bills received:

	25,000	
		25,000

Payments:

	23,500	
		23,500

The compound entry:

	25,000	
		23,500
		1,500

Solution. The two simple entries to record the expense and make payments are:

Phone Expense	25,000	
Expenses Payable		25,000

Expenses Payable	23,500	
Cash		23,500

Expenses payable increased by $1,500 during the year. The expense increases the liability by $25,000; payments reduce it by $23,500. In compound form, the entries are as follows:

Phone Expense	25,000	
Cash		23,500
Expenses Payable		1,500

Congratulations! Comfort with this exercise means that you understand both expenses payable and compound entries.

Exercise 4-6: Expenses Payable. The Big Bird Company has been in business for several years. At the beginning of the year, the Expenses Payable account for electricity was $50,000. During the year, the company received electric bills for $400,000 and paid $390,000. Show T-accounts to reflect the transactions relating to electricity use for the year. (Hint: utilities send bills when they provide services. Thus, the bill from the utility reflects an expense to Big Bird, the use of electric services.)

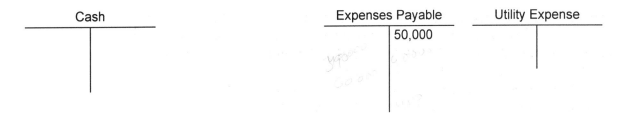

Solution. Since the company paid $10,000 less than the amount billed, the Expenses Payable account balance increases by this amount to $60,000. Big Bird received bills for $400,000 and presumably used services in the same amount. Thus, utility expense is $400,000. You could work this exercise using either two simple entries or one compound entry.

As two simple entries:

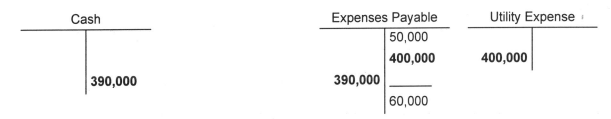

As one compound entry:

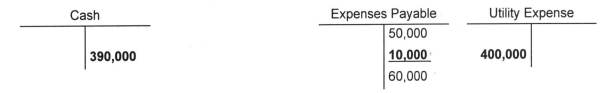

While it would have been easier to use journal entries for this problem, T-accounts help us visualize the relationships between the balance sheet and income statement. They also make it easy to calculate ending balances. Both journal entries and T-accounts help us learn the accounting system and analyze changes in accounts.

Interest Payable and Receivable

Interest receivable and payable accruals are also common. Loans typically earn interest on a continuous basis. The interest, however, may be paid only periodically.

Example: Interest Payable. The Sarah Corporation borrowed $100,000 on April 1 by issuing 10 percent bonds payable. The annual interest at 10 percent is $10,000. Following the usual custom, these bonds pay $5,000 interest twice per year. Since Sarah borrowed on April 1, semi-annual interest payments are due at the end of March and September.

On April 1 Year 1, Sarah makes the following entry to record the receipt of cash and loan payable:

Cash		Bonds Payable	
100,000			100,000

For the first interest payment at the end of September:

Cash		Bonds Payable		Interest Expense	
100,000			100,000		
	5,000			5,000	

At this point, three months remain to the end of the year.

In late December, Sarah accrues interest from September to the year end because the company used services (borrowed funds) until the end of the year. As a result, $2,500, the interest for three months, shows as an expense for the year and a liability on December 31:

Cash		Interest Payable		Bonds Payable		Interest Expense	
100,000					100,000		
	5,000					5,000	
95,000			2,500			**2,500**	
						7,500	

Thus, interest expense, the use of services from April 1 to December 31, is $7,500. Since the payment for Year 1 was only $5,000, $2,500 shows as interest payable, a liability. At the end of Year 1, interest expense is closed to Income Summary. Now we consider Year 2. At the beginning of Year 2, the Interest Expense account balance is zero. The liability accounts, however, are all permanent. Account balances for the liabilities on January 1, Year 2 are:

Interest Payable		Bonds Payable	
	2,500		100,000

At the end of March, the company pays interest and records two transactions. First, it accrues interest expense for the three-month period January through March. This amount is $2,500. Then, the company records the $5,000 payment:

Cash	Interest Payable	Bonds Payable	Interest Expense
	2,500	100,000	
	2,500		**2,500**
5,000	**5,000**		
	0		

In journal entry form with two single entries:

Interest Expense	2,500	
Interest Payable		2,500
Interest Payable	5,000	
Cash		5,000

Or, as a compound entry:

Interest Expense	2,500	
Interest Payable	2,500	
Cash		5,000

This exercise shows that you understand interest payable. Based on your understanding of interest payable, try to work the following interest receivable problem.

Exercise 4-7: Interest Revenue and Interest Receivable. The Sarah Corporation borrowed $100,000 on April 1 by issuing 10 percent bonds payable in the previous example. Now we learn that Michael Jackson was the lender. Michael bought all the bonds. His interest revenue is $5,000 every six months. He receives cash at the ends of March and September. Michael's accountant uses the same numbers as Sarah Corporation, the borrower. The initial transfer of cash to the Sarah Corporation is shown in the following accounts. Show T-account entries to record Michael's interest revenue and interest received for the first year.

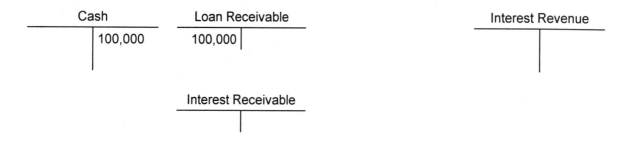

Solution

For the initial receipt of interest at the end of September:

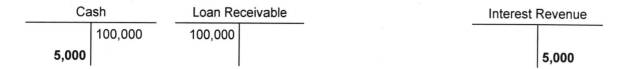

To record the accrual of three months of interest ($25,000) at the end of December:

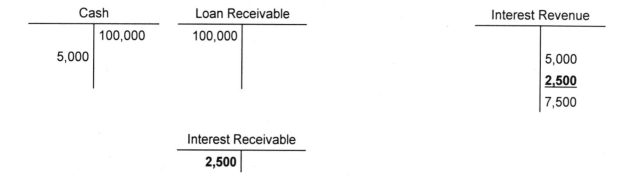

Interest revenue for providing services from April 1 to December 31 is $7,500. Since Michael receives only $5,000, his interest receivable at the end of the year is $2,500. This corresponds to the borrower's interest payable at the end of Year 1.

Exercise 4-8: Interest Receivable for the Second Year. In continuation of the previous exercise, develop and record the transactions for Year 2. We can ignore the Loan Receivable account since it does not change during Year 2.

Cash	Interest Receivable	Interest Revenue
	2,500	

Solution. In March of the second year, Michael records two transactions. First, he records $2,500 interest revenue for the period January through March. Then he records receipt of the $5,000 by debiting cash and crediting (reducing) the receivable. These transactions are:

Cash	Interest Receivable	Interest Revenue
	2,500	
	2,500	
5,000	_____ | **5,000**	**2,500**
	0	

In September, Michael records an additional $5,000 revenue and cash receipt. Then, on December 31, Michael reflects the accrual of three months interest revenue:

Cash	Interest Receivable	Interest Revenue
	2,500	
	2,500	2,500
5,000	_____ | 5,000	
	0	
5,000		**5,000**
	2,500	**2,500**
	2,500	

At this point, Michael's ending receivable is $2,500.

MAIN POINTS

Revenue and expense recognition does not always correspond to the timing of cash receipts and payments. Sellers of goods on account record accounts receivable and sales revenue. Buyers, in these cases record accounts payable. These receivables and payables are asset and liability accounts. This procedure permits firms to record revenue and purchases before the receipt or payment of cash.

Similar treatments apply to other transactions where cash collections or payments do not correspond to providing services or receiving services. Examples include receivables and payables for electricity, gas, and other utilities and for interest receivable.

APPENDIX TO CHAPTER 4— EXERCISES IN FINANCIAL ANALYSIS

These exercises provide additional practice working with concepts outlined in the main part of the chapter, introduce basic approaches to financial statement analysis, and help us to relate changes in various accounts with changes in cash. If you have difficulty with any of these exercises, review the topic in the main body of the chapter and try again.

Exercise A4-1: Accounts Payable. Businesses record Accounts Payable when they purchase goods on account and reduce Accounts Payable when they make payment. This exercise shows that an understanding of Accounts Payable provides information about other accounts such as inventory.

In this exercise, the beginning Accounts Payable balance is $80,000. During the year, the company pays $200,000 for inventory and ends with Accounts Payable of $110,000. The plant manager needs to know why the Inventory account balance is lower than expected and has asked us to calculate the amount of inventory purchased on account.

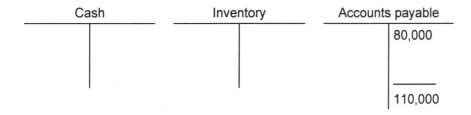

Solution. Inventory purchases were $230,000. Given the beginning and ending accounts payable, we can analyze the situation by first recording the disbursement of cash and reduction of payables. Then, we determine the increase to Accounts Payable. This is the cost of inventory purchases.

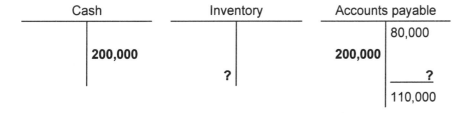

We know that Accounts Payable increase with inventory purchases. Therefore, we can replace the question marks with $230,000, the increase in payables and the amount of purchases.

Exercise A4-2: Wages Payable. Accounting for wages payable and accounts payable are very similar. The liability for wages payable increases with wage expense and decreases with payments to workers.

The Chocolate Pudding Corporation began and ended the year with the Wages Payable account balances shown in the following T-accounts. During the year wage expense was $400,000. How much did the Pudding Corporation pay its employees?

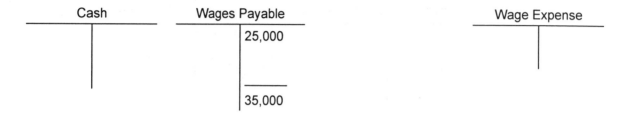

Solution. Payments to employees must have been $390,000. We know that the company initially records the $400,000 wages earned as both an expense and a liability. It then reduces the liability when it pays the workers.

We started with beginning wages payable of $25,000 and increased this when we recorded the $400,000 expense. Then, the only way to end the year with a $35,000 liability is to pay the workers $390,000. If we substitute other amounts for the payments, the ending liability will not be $35,000. In other words, nothing else works!

Cash		Wages Payable		Wage Expense	
			25,000		
			400,000	**400,000**	
390,000		**390,000**	———		
			35,000		

Exercise A4-3: Interest Receivable. This exercise tests our understanding of the Interest Receivable account. Receivables increase with interest revenue and decrease with receipts of cash.

The Muss Corporation begins the year with $4,000 of Interest Receivable. At the end of the year, the account balance is $4,400. Interest revenue for the year was $60,000. T-accounts are provided to help in your determination of the cash received from borrowers.

Cash	Interest Receivable	Interest Revenue
	4,000	
	4,400	

The cash received from borrowers was:

a. $59,600
b.   60,000
c.   60,400
d.   60,800
e.   64,400

Solution: A. The cash received from borrowers was $59,600. Given the $400 increase in the receivable, cash receipts are $400 less than interest revenue.

The following accounts show that interest receivable and interest revenue both increased by $60,000. Since the ending receivable balance is given as $4,400, interest receivable must have been reduced by $59,600.

CHAPTER 5

PAY NOW, EXPENSE LATER

(Costs in Advance of Expenses)

CHAPTER 5

PAY NOW, EXPENSE LATER
(Costs in Advance of Expenses)

Costs are amounts paid or to be paid for services. We already know about payments for salaries, electricity, or repairs that are recorded immediately as expenses to reflect the use of services. But, what about payments that relate to future accounting periods? For example, tenants sometimes pay their rent in advance. Accountants do not recognize expenses immediately in this case. Instead, they delay the recognition of expenses until the services are used.

This chapter illustrates three important categories of costs in advance. These are prepayments, long-lived assets, and inventories. Payments for these items occur as required during the year. Expenses, however, are typically entered as adjustments at the end of the accounting period.

PREPAYMENTS

Some payments made in advance of the use of services are referred to as prepayments. We now consider prepayments for rent and insurance.

Prepaid Rent

When tenants pay on January 1 for the use of space during the month, they are prepaying their rent. Prepaid rent is recorded as an asset, an item of value. An example follows:

Example: Prepaid Rent. In January our business signs a lease to open a store. The rental is $5,000 per month. Our landlord requires three months payment in advance -- $15,000. The entry to record the payment and acquisition of a valuable asset is:

Prepaid Rent	Cash		Rent Expense
15,000	15,000		

Recording the prepayment as an asset rather than as an expense accomplishes two objectives. First, the balance sheet shows an item of value -- the right to use the premises for three months. Second, the expense is not recognized until the services are used.

At the end of the first month, the use of services is recorded as follows:

Prepaid Rent		Cash		Rent Expense
15,000				
	5,000			5,000
10,000				

The accounts show that classification of the $15,000 payment, at this point, is divided. Part of the payment shows as rent expense. The remainder shows as an asset, prepaid rent.

This procedure continues for the second and third months until the entire prepaid rent balance is expensed. (In practice, rental agreements usually provide for prepaid rent balances to be maintained at all times. Thus, a second cash payment and an addition to prepaid rent will probably be required at the end of the first month.)

Exercise 5-1: Prepaid Rent. The preceding example considers the $15,000 advance payment of rent. This reflects rental costs of $5,000 per month for three months. After one month, the Prepaid Rent account balance is $10,000. Assuming no additional payments, use the following T-accounts and record entries for the next two months.

```
        Prepaid Rent                                    Rent Expense
     ─────────────────                            ─────────────────
      10,000 │                                            │
             │                                            │
             │                                            │
             │                                            │
             │                                            │
```

Solution

Beginning with a Prepaid Rent account balance of $10,000, the company expenses an additional $5,000 per month until the Prepaid Rent account balance is reduced to zero. Your T-account entries should look like the following:

```
        Prepaid Rent                                    Rent Expense
     ─────────────────                            ─────────────────
      10,000 │                                            │
      _____ │ 5,000                                5,000 │
       5,000 │                                            │
      _____ │ 5,000                                5,000 │
           0 │                                            │
```

Note that over the three month period, the expense totals $15,000. This is the same as the cash payment. Over the long run, the cash paid for services always becomes an expense.

Prepaid Insurance

Insurance companies usually require policy holders to pay premiums in advance. The payments are initially recorded as Prepaid Insurance, an asset. This asset is then reduced gradually as time passes and the insurance provides protection. Accounting for prepaid insurance and rent follow the same procedure. If you understand prepaid rent accounting, you should be able to account for prepaid insurance.

Exercise 5-2: Prepaid Insurance. The Carson Company purchases an insurance policy for $12,000 on January 1. The policy provides for a full year of liability insurance. On January 1 the entry is:

Prepaid Insurance	Cash	Insurance Expense
12,000	**12,000**	

Record the transactions to adjust the accounts at the ends of January and February. Then, show the Prepaid Insurance account balance at the end of two months.

Prepaid Insurance	Cash	Insurance Expense
12,000	12,000	

Solution

Insurance expense is $1,000 per month ($12,000 annual/ 12 months). Over the two month period, prepaid insurance decreases from $12,000 to $10,000 as follows:

Prepaid Insurance	Cash	Insurance Expense
12,000	12,000	
1,000		**1,000**
11,000		
1,000		**1,000**
10,000		

Exercise 5-3: Prepaid Insurance. The Witch Corporation renews its one-year insurance policy at the beginning of July. The policy amount is $60,000 with the entire amount payable in advance on July 1. Show all entries for July, August, and September.

Prepaid Insurance	Cash	Insurance Expense

Solution

Since the 12 month policy is for $60,000, insurance expense will be $5,000 per month. The accounts should show:

Prepaid Insurance	Cash	Insurance Expense
60,000	60,000	
5,000		5,000
55,000		
5,000		5,000
50,000		
5,000		5,000
45,000		

The $45,000 ending Prepaid Insurance account balance provides for nine more months of service at $5,000 per month. At the end of 12 months, the expense at $5,000 per month will total $60,000. The cumulative expense must equal the $60,000 payment.

Exercise 5-4: Prepaid Accounts. We know that prepaid asset accounts increase with payments and decrease with expenses, the use of services.

The Foam Corporation begins the year with $12,000 in prepaid insurance. During the year, Foam pays an additional $50,000 for insurance. Insurance expense during the year is $60,000. What is the ending balance in the Prepaid Insurance account?

Solution

The ending Prepaid Insurance account balance is $2,000. This account increases by the $50,000 payment and decreases by the $60,000 expense as shown in the following entries.

Since prepaid insurance reflects payments to the insurance company, we increase the Prepaid Insurance account when we make the $50,000 payment. Then, we decrease this account over time as we benefit from the insurance. In this case, the use of services is given as $60,000. A compound entry leads to the same end result. Prepaid insurance decreases by $10,000 because payments for the year are less than the $60,000 amount of insurance services used.

Prepaid Insurance		Cash		Insurance Expense
12,000				
	10,000	50,000		60,000
2,000				

LONG-LIVED ASSETS

Long-lived assets are a second important category of costs in advance of expenses. When property with a long expected life is acquired, the initial cost is recorded as an asset. Expenses are recorded later through a process called depreciation. Depreciation is just an allocation process which records expense gradually over the period of expected benefit.

Example: Depreciation Expense. The Jones Company purchases a building for $200,000. This building has an expected life of 20 years.

Initially, the $200,000 cost is recorded as an asset. The expense is recorded later as depreciation. Accountants usually calculate depreciation expense by apportioning the asset's cost over its expected life as follows:

Annual depreciation expense = Amount to be depreciated / Expected life

= $200,000 / 20 years = $10,000 per year

Depreciation reduces income and also reduces the asset balance (as the asset is considered to be used). Accountants show the reduction in the asset in a separate account called Accumulated Depreciation.

Accumulated Depreciation

Accumulated depreciation is the cumulative depreciation recorded since the asset was acquired. An example follows:

Example: The Accumulated Depreciation Account. The Fried Chicken Company purchases a $200,000 building with expected life 20 years. Entries to record the purchase and the first year's depreciation expense are:

Building		Accumulated Depreciation		Cash		Depreciation Expense	
200,000			10,000	200,000		10,000	

The company records an asset when it buys the building. Then, the business makes an adjusting entry to record the $10,000 expense and credit to Accumulated Depreciation. Whenever depreciation expense is recorded, an equal amount is credited to Accumulated Depreciation.

Comparing balances in the Building and Accumulated Depreciation accounts, gives a net amount of $190,000. This is referred to as 'book value,' or 'carrying value.' Some accountants also refer to the 'building, net.' We'll refer to the net amount as book value.

Building	$200,000	
Accumulated Depreciation	10,000	
Book Value	$190,000	

Accumulated Depreciation is called a contra account because the balance is opposite that of the long-lived asset account. Accumulated depreciation has a right-side balance while the primary account, the building, has a left-side balance. Both accounts are permanent accounts.

The Accumulated Depreciation account balance grows each year with each year's depreciation expense. Accumulated depreciation, however, will never exceed the balance in the building or other primary account. Depreciation, as indicated earlier, just assigns the expected cost of ownership over the period of expected benefit. Once this occurs, depreciation stops.

Exercise 5-5: Accumulated Depreciation. The following accounts show balances for the Fried Chicken Company's Building and Accumulated Depreciation accounts at the end of Year 1. Show the Year 2 and 3 entries to depreciation expense and accumulated depreciation. Then, calculate the building's book value at the end of Year 3.

Building	Accumulated Depreciation	Depreciation Expense
200,000	10,000	

Solution

The building's book value at the end of Year 3 is $170,000.

Accumulated depreciation increases at the rate of $10,000 per year. At the end of Year 3, the Accumulated Depreciation account balance is $30,000. The book value, then, must be $170,000 ($200,000 - $30,000). Year 2 and 3 entries to record depreciation expense and accumulated depreciation are:

Building	Accumulated Depreciation	Depreciation Expense
200,000	10,000	
	10,000	**10,000**
	10,000	**10,000**
	30,000	

After 17 more years, accumulated depreciation will be $200,000. Then, depreciation stops as the building is fully depreciated.

Exercise 5-6: Depreciation Expense and Accumulated Depreciation. The Baked Burger Company buys new kitchen equipment with a 10 year expected life for $80,000. Determine the annual depreciation expense and the equipment's book value at the end of Year 5. The following relationship and T-accounts should be helpful:

Annual depreciation expense = Amount to be depreciated / Expected life

=

Equipment	Accumulated Depreciation		Depreciation Expense
80,000			

To calculate the book value:

Equipment	$80,000
Accumulated Depreciation	_____
Book Value	

Solution

The annual depreciation expense is $8,000 and the book value at the end of Year 5 is $40,000. We calculate depreciation using the following relationship:

$$\text{Annual depreciation expense} = \text{Amount to be depreciated} / \text{Expected life}$$

$$= \$80,000 / 10 \text{ years} = \$8,000 \text{ per year}$$

Entries to record depreciation expense and accumulated depreciation are:

Equipment		Accumulated Depreciation		Depreciation Expense	
80,000			8,000		8,000
			8,000		8,000
			8,000		8,000
			8,000		8,000
			8,000		8,000
			40,000		

The equipment's book value is the equipment account less the accumulated depreciation:

Equipment	$80,000
Accumulated Depreciation	40,000
Book Value	$40,000

Sale of Long-lived Assets

When businesses sell property for cash, the sellers record the cash and remove the property from the books. Initially, we consider the purchase and sale of land. Land is not depreciated because unlike trucks or machines, it doesn't ordinarily lose its usefulness.

Example: Purchase and Sale of Land. The Lilien Corporation purchases land for $500,000 to build a small shopping plaza. Several years later, Lilien decides not to build and sells the land for $500,000. The purchase is recorded as:

Land	500,000	
Cash		500,000

This entry is then reversed on sale of the land for $500,000.

Cash	500,000	
Land		500,000

In T-account form:

Land		Cash	
500,000			500,000
	500,000	500,000	
0		0	

Gains on Sale

In practice, it isn't usual to buy and sell at the same price because asset values change over time. This leads to gains or losses on sale. Gains are recorded when selling prices exceed book values. Losses mean that selling prices are less than book values.

Example: Gains on Sale. The Iceberg Corporation purchases land for $500,000 and plans to expand its factory. Three years later, the company closes the factory and sells the land for $650,000. Iceberg recognizes a $150,000 gain on sale. This gain is the difference between the selling price and book value as shown in the following accounts:

Land		Cash		Gain on Sale	
500,000			500,000		
	500,000	650,000			150,000
0		0			

In journal entry form:

Cash	650,000	
Land		500,000
Gain on Sale		150,000

The Interpretation of Gains and Losses on Sale

Gains and losses increase or decrease income. In this respect they resemble revenues and expenses. Income statements, however, report gains and losses separately because they are usually one-time items. For example, when a store records revenue, we ordinarily expect similar revenue in the future. This is not the case for gains on sale. Once the business sells land, investments, or equipment, the items are gone. There will not be any future gains on sale from these particular items. In fact, it isn't unusual for a company to report gains in one year and losses in the following year. The following income statement shows a typical presentation of a gain on sale:

Fruitcup Incorporated
Income for the Year ended December 31, 19x1

Sales Revenue		$400,000
Expenses		
Cost of Goods Sold	$300,000	
Other Expenses	70,000	370,000
Income From Operations		$30,000
Gain on Sale of Equipment		**60,000**
Income Before Taxes		$90,000

Gains and losses are closed to Income Summary using the same procedure applicable to revenues and expenses.

Exercise 5-7: Loss on Sale. The Torpedo Corporation purchased land for $600,000 and now sells the property for $250,000. When selling prices are less than book value, accountants record losses. Determine the loss on sale and show T-accounts for the purchase and sale transactions.

Solution

Since the selling price is $350,000 less than book value, Torpedo Corporation shows a $350,000 loss on sale. The entries to record the purchase and sale are:

In the sale transaction, the Land account is reduced by the land's original cost. This is necessary since the company no longer has the property. Cash increases by the $250,000 selling price. The loss is the difference between the selling price and the book value -- $600,000 less $250,000. In journal entry form, the transaction is:

Cash	250,000	
Loss on Sale	350,000	
Land		600,000

How can we be sure that the $350,000 amount is a loss rather than a gain? The loss account has a left-side entry which reduces equity. Mechanically, losses work the same way as expenses. It's just that the interpretation differs.

The Sale of Depreciable Property

We now consider the sale of depreciable property. The same principles apply to the sale of land and depreciable property. With depreciable property, however, an additional account is involved. When equipment or other depreciable property is sold, accountants close both the asset and associated Accumulated Depreciation accounts.

Exercise 5-8: Review of Accounting for Depreciable Property. The Fuss Corporation pays $200,000 for equipment with an expected life of five years. Fuss continues to use the equipment during Year 6. Depreciation, however, stops after five years. At this point, the Accumulated Depreciation account balance equals the cost of the equipment. This review exercise concerns entries to record depreciation expense. Use the T-accounts shown below.

Equipment	Accumulated Depreciation	Cash	Depreciation Expense
200,000			

Solution

Entries for the six year period are as follows:

Equipment	Accumulated Depreciation	Cash	Depreciation Expense
200,000	40,000		40,000
	40,000		40,000
	40,000		40,000
	40,000		40,000
	40,000		40,000
	<u>0</u>		0
	200,000		

At the end of Year 5, the equipment's book value is zero. The equipment is now fully depreciated and consequently, it is not possible to record additional depreciation expense in Year 6.

Depreciation Expense and the Cash Account

Note that in the previous exercise, you did not record any entries to Cash when you depreciated the equipment. This illustrates an important concept. Depreciation is purely an allocation of previously recorded costs. While it may be an important determinant of income, depreciation has absolutely no impact upon the Cash account.

Exercise 5-9: Gain or Loss on Sale. In the previous review exercise, the Fuss Corporation bought equipment for $200,000 and depreciated it to zero book value over five years. Now, we learn that Fuss sells the equipment early in Year 7 for $80,000. Calculate the gain on sale by comparing the $80,000 cash received on sale to the Year 7 book value. Then, record the entry for the sale. Be sure to remove the Accumulated Depreciation account from the books when you remove the Equipment account.

Selling price	_____
Book value	_____
Gain on Sale	_____

The journal entry is:

Cash	_____	
Accumulated Depreciation	_____	
Equipment		_____
Gain on Sale		_____

Starting with the beginning balances shown below, update the T-accounts for Year 7 by recording the information in the preceding journal entry.

Equipment	Accumulated Depreciation	Cash	Gain on Sale
200,000	200,000		

Solution

Fuss calculates an $80,000 gain as follows:

Selling price	$80,000
Book value	0
Gain on Sale	$80,000

The journal entry is:

Cash	80,000	
Accumulated Depreciation	200,000	
Equipment		200,000
Gain on Sale		80,000

We debit cash to show receipt of a valuable asset. Accumulated Depreciation is also debited to offset the amount shown in this contra-account. (We can't show accumulated depreciation on the books for an item that we no longer have.) Then, equipment is credited to remove the asset from the books. The gain can be calculated as the missing number necessary to ensure that debits equal credits.

The Year 7 T-account entries are:

Equipment		Accumulated Depreciation		Cash		Gain on Sale	
200,000			200,000				
	200,000	**200,000**		**80,000**			**80,000**

The Sale of Depreciable Property Before the End of its Life

If the book value is not zero at the time of sale, the gain will differ from the selling price. The next exercise assumes that the property is sold before it is fully depreciated.

Exercise 5-10: Accounting for Depreciable Property. The Fuss Corporation buys equipment costing $200,000 and begins to depreciate the property over five years. Early in Year 4, before depreciation is recorded, Fuss sells the equipment for $110,000.

First, calculate the book value at the time of sale. To do this, refer to entries up to the time of sale (reproduced below). Then, determine the gain on sale. Finally, record the entry for the sale.

Equipment		Accumulated Depreciation		Cash		Depreciation Expense	
200,000			40,000	200,000		40,000	
			40,000			40,000	
			40,000			40,000	
			120,000				

Selling price   _____

Book value   _____

Gain on Sale   _____

The journal entry to record the sale is:

Cash   _____

Accumulated Depreciation   _____

       Equipment   _____

       Gain on Sale   _____

Starting with the beginning balances shown below, update the T-accounts for Year 4.

Equipment		Accumulated Depreciation		Cash		Gain on Sale	
200,000			120,000				

Solution

In this case, Fuss calculates a $30,000 gain as follows:

Selling price	$110,000
Book value	80,000
Gain on Sale	$30,000

The company shows a $110,000 debit to record the receipt of cash. It also debits Accumulated Depreciation for $120,000, the amount on the books at the time of sale. Crediting Equipment for its $200,000 cost removes this account from the books. The gain can also be determined as the missing number necessary to complete the following entry:

Cash	110,000	
Accumulated Depreciation	120,000	
Equipment		200,000
Gain on Sale		30,000

And, the T-accounts show:

Equipment		Accumulated Depreciation		Cash		Gain on Sale	
200,000			120,000				
	200,000	120,000		110,000			30,000

Exercise 5-11: Loss on the Sale of Depreciable Property. The Sprat Corporation buys a new truck for $300,000 and begins to depreciate the property over three years. Early in Year 3, Sprat sells the truck for $70,000.

First, calculate the annual depreciation and record depreciation expense for two years (to the beginning of Year 3). Then, determine the loss on sale. Finally, record the entry for the sale.

Annual depreciation expense = Amount to be depreciated / Expected life

=

T-account entries for the first two years:

Truck	Accumulated Depreciation	Cash	Depreciation Expense

Find the loss by comparing the selling price and book value.

Selling price	_____
Book value	_____
Loss on Sale	_____

The entry to record the sale is:

Cash	_____	
Accumulated Depreciation	_____	
Loss on Sale	_____	
Truck		_____

T-account entries to record the sale of the truck early in Year 3:

Truck		Accumulated Depreciation		Cash	Loss on Sale
300,000			200,000		

Solution

Sprat has a $30,000 loss on sale because the selling price does not equal the truck's book value.

Annual depreciation expense = Amount to be depreciated / Expected life

Annual depreciation expense = $300,000 / 3 years = $100,000 per year

After two years, Sprat's accumulated depreciation is $200,000 and the book value is $100,000. This leads to a loss on sale as follows:

Selling price	$70,000
Book value	100,000
Loss on Sale	$30,000

The journal entry to record the sale is:

Cash	70,000	
Accumulated Depreciation	200,000	
Loss on Sale	30,000	
Truck		300,000

And, the T-account entries for Year 3 are as follows:

Truck		Accumulated Depreciation		Cash		Loss on Sale	
300,000			200,000				
	300,000	**200,000**		**70,000**		**30,000**	

Residual Value

Residual value is the amount received when the asset is sold. This is also called salvage value. Accountants always estimate expected residual value. If we buy property for $500,000 and expect to sell it for $200,000, the expected residual value is $200,000. In this case, the expected net cost of ownership is only $300,000 ($500,000 purchase price less $200,000 expected selling price). Only the expected net cost is subject to depreciation. We'll see that this approach always reduces income, in the long run, by the net cost of ownership.

Example: Depreciable Property with Residual Value. The Summer Corporation pays $500,000 for a computer. Its expected life is three years and the expected residual value (future selling price) is $200,000. During Year 4, Summer sells the computer for $200,000.

Since the cost will be partly offset by the $200,000 estimated residual value, the expected net cost of ownership is only $300,000. We depreciate this amount.

Annual depreciation expense = Amount to be depreciated / Expected life

= (Cost-Residual value) / Expected life

= ($500,000 - $200,000) / 3 years

= $100,000 per year

With annual depreciation of $100,000, accumulated depreciation will total $300,000 after three years. The book value, then, will be $200,000 (equal to the expected selling price). Thus, a sale at exactly $200,000 will not result in gain or loss. The following T-accounts show the transactions to the time of sale.

Computer	Accumulated Depreciation	Cash	Depreciation Expense
500,000		500,000	
	100,000		100,000
	100,000		100,000
	100,000		100,000
	300,000		

At the time of sale, the journal entry is:

Cash	200,000	
Accumulated Depreciation	300,000	
Equipment		500,000

Exercise 5-12: Depreciable Property with Residual Value and a Gain on Sale. The Quail Company pays $50,000 for new machinery. This machinery has a four-year expected life and a $20,000 expected residual value. Consequently, only $30,000 is subject to depreciation. Quail sells the machinery for $38,000 early in Year 3. Calculate the annual depreciation. Then, record depreciation entries for two years. Finally, record the sale for Year 3 .

Annual depreciation expense = Amount to be depreciated / Expected life

= (Cost-Residual value) / Expected life

=

T-account entries for the first two years.

Machinery	Accumulated Depreciation	Cash	Depreciation Expense

Compare the Machinery and Accumulated Depreciation accounts to determine the gain on sale.

Selling price   _____
Book value   _____
Gain on Sale   _____

The entry for the sale is:

Cash   _____
Accumulated Depreciation   _____
Machinery   _____
Gain on Sale   _____

Solution

Quail records a $3,000 gain on sale. The company's annual depreciation expense is:

$$\text{Annual depreciation expense} = \text{Amount to be depreciated} / \text{Expected life}$$

$$= (\text{Cost-Residual value}) / \text{Expected life}$$

$$= (\$50,000 - \$20,000) / 4 \text{ years}$$

$$= \$7,500 \text{ per year}$$

After recording depreciation for the first two years, the T-accounts early in Year 3 should appear as follows:

Machinery	Accumulated Depreciation	Cash	Depreciation Expense
50,000		50,000	
	7,500		**7,500**
	7,500		**7,500**
	15,000		

Comparing the Machinery and Accumulated Depreciation accounts results in a $35,000 book value ($50,000 for machinery less $15,000 for accumulated depreciation). The gain on the $38,000 sale is:

Selling price	$38,000
Book value	35,000
Gain on Sale	$3,000

Quail record the sale as follows:

Cash	38,000	
Accumulated Depreciation	15,000	
Machinery		50,000
Gain on Sale		3,000

INVENTORIES

Inventories are a third important case of costs in advance of expenses. In some respects, this is a review topic since it was included earlier in transactions exercises. We learned that the costs of items manufactured or purchased for resale are recorded as assets. Inventory is reduced and expenses are recorded as the goods are sold. The cost of goods sold is recognized at the time of sale because this is when the ownership of inventory transfers to the buyer. Services are assumed to be used at this time.

Example: Inventory. The Techie Corporation buys 100 computers for $2,500 each. During the year, it sells 80 of these items to customers. This means that 20 computers remain in inventory at year-end. The entry to record purchases is:

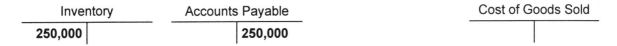

Inventory	Accounts Payable		Cost of Goods Sold
250,000 |	| **250,000**		|

Techie now has 100 items available for sale at a cost of $250,000. For accounting purposes, the cost of goods available breaks into two components. These are ending inventory and the cost of goods sold.

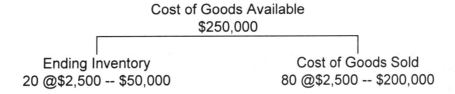

Cost of Goods Available
$250,000

Ending Inventory	Cost of Goods Sold
20 @$2,500 -- $50,000	80 @$2,500 -- $200,000

Since 80 percent of the computers are sold, 80 percent of the original purchase price is expensed. The remaining $50,000 will be expensed when all computers are sold. The entry to adjust the inventory and record the cost of goods sold is:

Inventory		Cost of Goods Sold
250,000 |		|
| **200,000**		**200,000** |
50,000 |		

After the first year in business, the cost of goods available will consist of beginning inventory plus the cost of purchases. The next exercise considers the usual ongoing inventory situation.

Exercise 5-13: Inventories and the Cost of Goods Sold. The Zoo-at-Home Company, a large pet store, began the year with 100 puppies each costing $20. During the year, the company bought 1,000 additional puppies for $20 each. This means that 1,100 puppies are available for sale. Of the 1,100 puppies available for sale, 1,050 were sold during the year. Your challenge is to find the cost of goods available. Then determine the cost of ending inventory and cost of goods sold. Finally, make the appropriate entries in the T-accounts.

First , determine the cost of goods available for sale.

	Number of Puppies	Total Cost
Beginning Inventory	100	_____
Purchases	1,000	_____
Cost of Goods Available	1,100	_____

Then, divide the cost of goods available into its components.

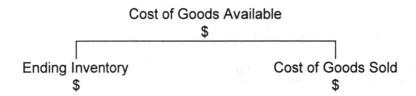

Cost of Goods Available
$

Ending Inventory
$

Cost of Goods Sold
$

Finally, record entries for the purchase and sale of inventories.

Inventory	Accounts Payable	Cost of Goods Sold
2,000		

Solution

The cost of goods available for sale is.

	Number of Puppies	Total Cost @$20 each
Beginning Inventory	100	$2,000
Purchases	1,000	20,000
Cost of Goods Available	1,100	$22,000

Components of the cost of goods available for sale are:

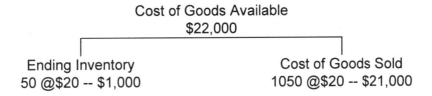

Cost of Goods Available
$22,000

Ending Inventory
50 @$20 -- $1,000

Cost of Goods Sold
1050 @$20 -- $21,000

Zoo-at-Home's T-accounts are as follows:

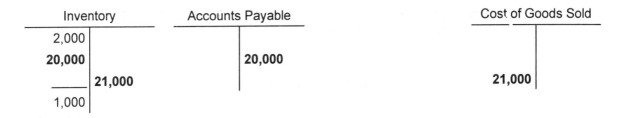

These accounts show that beginning inventory and accounts payable increase with the $20,000 purchase of inventory. Inventory then decreases to reflect the $21,000 cost of goods sold.

The following exercise is similar to the previous one. You may wish to skip it if you're comfortable with the Zoo-at-Home Company exercise.

Exercise 5-14: Inventories and the Cost of Goods Sold. PowerBall, Incorporated sells a number of products including tennis rackets. The company began the year with 125 rackets costing $100 each. During the year, PowerBall bought 500 rackets at the same price. At the end of the year, only 25 rackets remain in inventory. Calculate the cost of goods sold and cost of ending inventory and record these entries in the accounts.

Always begin with the cost of goods available for sale.

	Number of Items	Total Cost
Beginning Inventory	125	_____
Purchases	500	_____
Cost of Goods Available	625	_____

Then, divide the cost of goods available into its components.

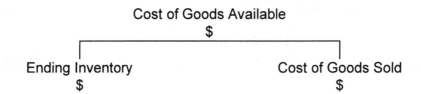

Your T-account entries to record the purchase and sale of inventory are:

Solution

The cost of goods available for sale is.

	Number of Items	Total Cost @$100
Beginning Inventory	125	$12,500
Purchases	500	50,000
Cost of Goods Available	625	$62,500

Components of the cost of goods available are:

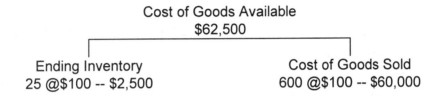

Cost of Goods Available
$62,500

Ending Inventory
25 @$100 -- $2,500

Cost of Goods Sold
600 @$100 -- $60,000

PowerBall's T-accounts show:

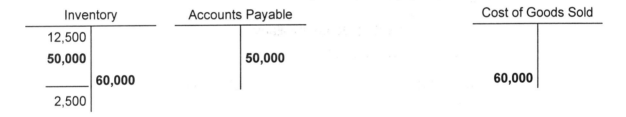

Inventory		Accounts Payable		Cost of Goods Sold	
12,500					
50,000			50,000		
	60,000			60,000	
2,500					

MAIN POINTS

Prepayments

Prepaid assets are recorded in the accounts when businesses pay for services before the services are actually received. The accounting procedure serves two purposes. First, the balance sheet shows an item of value -- the right to use services in the future. Second, the expense is recognized when the services are used.

With any prepayment situation, the amount paid eventually becomes an expense.

Long-Lived Assets

Property with a long expected life is initially recorded as an asset. The expense, which comes later, is called depreciation.

Depreciation is an allocation process which provides for recording expense gradually over the period of expected benefit. Over the long run, depreciation expense should equal the net cost of ownership. Depreciation expense reduces income and also reduces the book value of assets. Depreciation expense, however, does not reduce cash.

The reduction in the asset is shown separately in an account called Accumulated Depreciation. This account grows each year with cumulative depreciation expense.

Accumulated Depreciation is called a contra account because the balance is opposite to that of the primary account. Comparing the balances in the asset and Accumulated Depreciation accounts gives a net amount referred to as "book value" or "carrying value."

When property is sold for cash, the seller records cash and removes the item from the books. Both the asset and Accumulated Depreciation accounts must be removed from the books when depreciable property is sold.

Property sales usually result in gains or losses. These are temporary accounts which are closed to income summary.

Residual value is the amount received when the asset is sold. Only the cost less residual value is subject to depreciation. This approach always reduces income, in the long run, by the net cost of ownership.

Inventory

Inventory purchases are not expensed until the time of sale. This is when the use of services occurs.

The cost of goods available for sale is the cost of beginning inventory plus the cost of purchases. It has two components. One is the cost of ending inventory.   The second is the cost of goods sold.

APPENDIX TO CHAPTER 5– EXERCISES IN FINANCIAL ANALYSIS

Exercise A5-1: Prepaid Accounts. This exercise provides practice in working with changes in prepaid accounts to determine the amount paid for new insurance. Investors, lenders, and other financial statement users are concerned with cash because cash repays loans and pays dividends on investments. Understanding which events increase and decrease account balances permits us to determine cash paid for insurance and other items that are not disclosed in the financial statements.

The Good Health Corporation begins the year with $22,000 in prepaid insurance. During the year, insurance expense is $100,000 and the ending Prepaid Insurance account balance is $32,000. How much was paid for insurance this year? (Hint: First show the entry for insurance expense and the reduction of prepaid insurance. Then, determine the amount that the company added to Prepaid Insurance.)

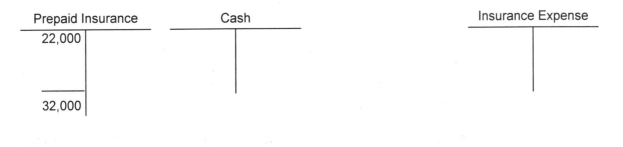

Solution

Payments for insurance were $110,000. The key to this problem is understanding that prepaid asset accounts increase with payments and decrease with expenses. We know that the Prepaid Insurance account was reduced by $100,000 and that the ending balance is $32,000. The challenge is to solve for the question marks.

The corporation must have added $110,000 to Prepaid Insurance. Good Health Corporation began the year with $22,000 in prepaid insurance. During the year, the company paid $110,000 to the insurance company and used services worth $100,000. This leaves the ending Prepaid Insurance account balance at $32,000 as shown in the following accounts:

Exercise A5-2: Prepaid Accounts. This exercise is similar to the previous one. Remember that prepaid insurance increases with payments and decreases with insurance expense.

The Trail Corporation begins the year with $15,000 in prepaid insurance. During the year, the company paid $90,000 to the insurance company and the ending Prepaid Insurance account balance is $5,000. What was the insurance expense for the year?

Prepaid Insurance	Cash	Insurance Expense
15,000		
5,000		

Solution

The insurance expense was $100,000. Some of the beginning prepaid insurance was used. Therefore, the expense exceeded the $90,000 amount paid.

Given that the Prepaid Insurance account initially increased by $90,000 (the payments) and the ending balance is $5,000, the expense must have been $100,000. Put differently, the only way to start with the $15,000 Prepaid Insurance account balance, pay $90,000 for insurance, and end with Prepaid Insurance of $5,000, is to incur insurance expense of $100,000. The following accounts show the $90,000 addition to Prepaid Insurance (the payment) and the $100,000 reduction for insurance expense.

Prepaid Insurance		Cash	Insurance Expense
15,000			
90,000		**90,000**	
	100,000		100,000
5,000			

Exercise A5-3: Equipment and Accumulated Depreciation Account Relationships. This exercise provides practice with Equipment and Accumulated Depreciation account relationships. It also shows how analysts can use asset and Accumulated Depreciation account relationships to develop information not provided directly in the accounts.

Remember that the Equipment account increases with purchases and decreases when the equipment is sold. The Accumulated Depreciation account increases with depreciation expense. When old equipment is sold, the accumulated depreciation to date is removed from the Accumulated Depreciation account. This first exercise is a warm-up in that it involves only two trucks.

The Windup Company began the year with one delivery truck. During the year, the depreciation expense recorded for the truck was $6,000. At the end of the year, Windup sold the truck and recognized a gain on sale of $4,000. Then, the company bought a new truck. The following T-accounts show the beginning and ending balances for the Truck and Accumulated Depreciation accounts. Our challenge is to calculate the amount received on the sale of the old truck and the cost of the new truck.

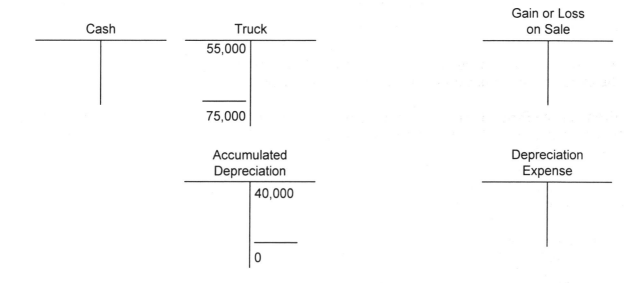

Solution

The cash received from the sale of the old truck was $13,000. The new truck cost $75,000. First, record the depreciation expense as follows:

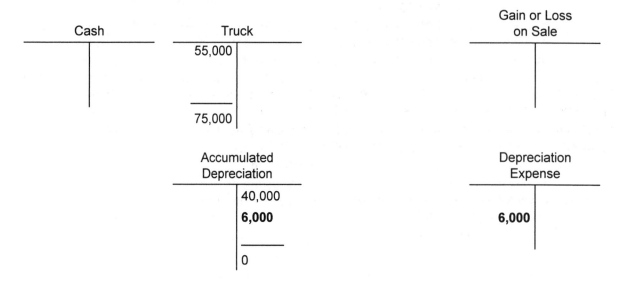

Cash	Truck	Gain or Loss on Sale
	55,000	
	75,000	

Accumulated Depreciation	Depreciation Expense
40,000	
6,000	6,000
0	

Additional depreciation expense brings the Accumulated Depreciation account balance to $46,000. We know that accumulated depreciation must be reduced to zero when the truck is sold. We also know that the Truck account must be reduced to zero. The entry to record the sale has four parts. Of these, we know three as follows:

Cash	?	
Accumulated Depreciation	46,000	
Truck		55,000
Gain on Sale		4,000

Given the preceding analysis, the cash received on the sale must have been $13,000. This is necessary for the debits to equal the credits.

Cash	13,000	
Accumulated Depreciation	46,000	
Truck		55,000
Gain on Sale		4,000

Another approach is to calculate the old truck's book value. Comparing the $55,000 cost and $46,000 accumulated depreciation gives a $9,000 book value. Then, the selling price has to be $13,0000 to provide a $4,000 gain on sale.

Selling price	$13,000
Book value	9,000
Gain on Sale	$4,000

We know the company paid $75,000 for the new truck because this is the only way that the Truck account can show a $75,000 ending balance. (The company debited the Truck account and credited Cash when it purchased the new truck for $75,000.) T-account entries to reflect the sale of the old truck and purchase of the new truck are as follows:

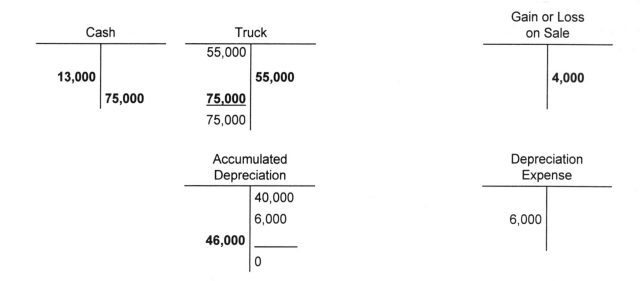

Exercise A5-4: **Accumulated Depreciation.** The Foster Corporation's Accumulated Depreciation account began the year with a $50,000 balance and ended with a $60,000 balance. Depreciation expense for the year was $230,000. Foster sold long-lived assets during the year. How much depreciation was accumulated on the items that the company sold?

Hint: Remember that accumulated depreciation increases with depreciation expense. The account decreases by the depreciation accumulated on items sold during the year. T-accounts can be very helpful with this type problem.

Since you know the beginning accumulated depreciation and the increase, the primary challenge is to calculate the entry to accumulated depreciation made on the sale of long-lived assets.

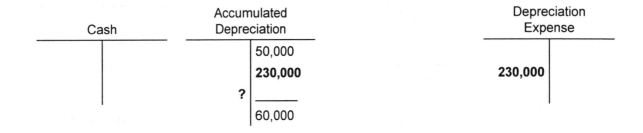

Solution

The accumulated depreciation applicable to the equipment sold was $220,000. This is the most likely cause of the change in the Accumulated Depreciation account balance. Substituting in the following set of accounts demonstrates that reducing Accumulated Depreciation by $220,000 provides the $60,000 ending Accumulated Depreciation account balance.

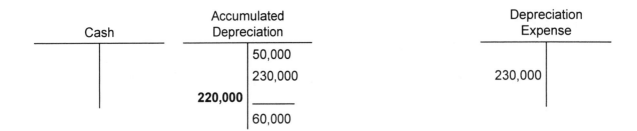

Exercise A5-5: Equipment and Accumulated Depreciation Account Relationships. This exercise is more realistic and more challenging that the earlier truck example because there are multiple assets and only some of the old items are sold during the year.

The Dropit Express Company began the year with several delivery trucks. During the year, depreciation expense was $60,000. At the end of the year, Dropit sold trucks which originally cost $48,000. The gain on sale was $15,000. Then, the company bought new trucks. The following T-accounts show the beginning and ending balances for the Truck and Accumulated Depreciation accounts. How much did the company receive on the sale of the old trucks? What was the cost of the new trucks?

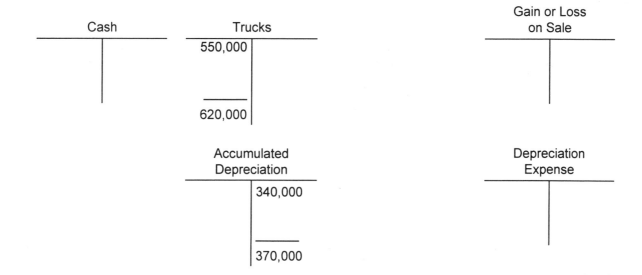

Solution

The cash received from the sale of the old trucks was $33,000. Dropit bought new trucks for $118,000. First, record the depreciation expense.

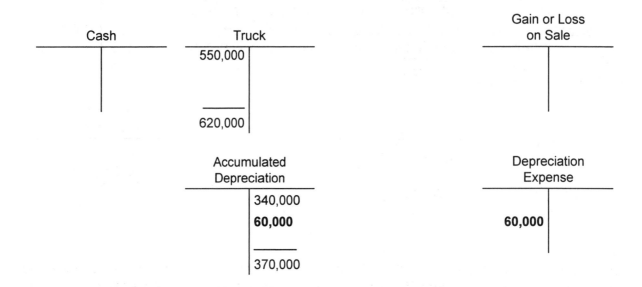

At this point, the beginning accumulated depreciation and $60,000 increase total $400,000. Since the ending balance is only $370,000, we know that the account was reduced by $30,000. The most likely reason is the removal of the depreciation accumulated on the trucks that were sold. Therefore, we know that the accumulated depreciation on the trucks that were sold was $30,000. This permits us to develop the following journal entry:

Cash	?	
Accumulated Depreciation	30,000	
Trucks		48,000
Gain on Sale		15,000

This tells us that the cash received on the sale must have been $33,000. Now, the entry balances as follows:

Cash	33,000	
Accumulated Depreciation	30,000	
Trucks		48,000
Gain on Sale		15,000

At this point, we can record the preceding journal entry information in the T-accounts:

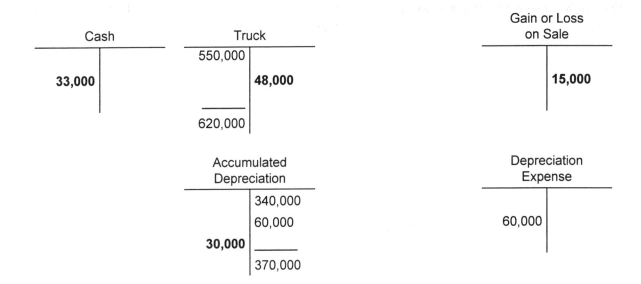

Now, we've explained everything except the Truck account. This account has a $502,000 balance after removing the cost of the old trucks that were sold. Since the ending balance is $620,000, we know that the company bought new trucks for $118,000. If you debit the Truck account for this amount, you'll have the correct ending balance.

Exercise A5-6: Plant and Equipment Accounts. This exercise incorporates the same concepts as the preceding one. While the approach is the same, the information that is given and the information that need to be determined differ.

The BeGone Company's beginning and ending Equipment and Accumulated Depreciation account balances for the year are shown below in T-accounts. During the year, the company bought equipment for $100,000. Depreciation expense for the year was $40,000. Also during the year, the company received $50,000 from the sale of old equipment. After recording the purchase and depreciation expense calculate the gain or loss on sale by completing the journal entry for the sale. Finally, show the various entries in the T-accounts.

Cash	Equipment		Gain or Loss on Sale
	400,000		
	470,000		

	Accumulated Depreciation		Depreciation Expense
	120,000		
	135,000		

Cash	_____
Accumulated Depreciation	_____
Equipment	_____
Gain on Sale	_____

Solution

The gain on sale must be $45,000. First, record the purchase of new equipment and depreciation expense for the year. This prepares the books for the entry on sale of the old equipment.

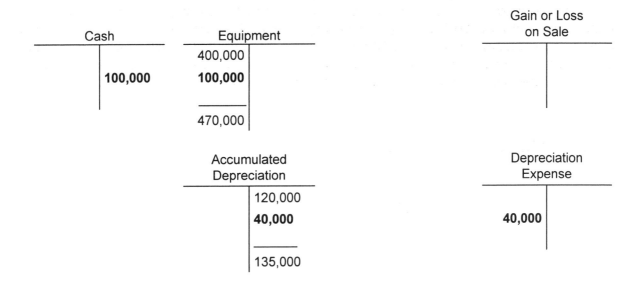

Then, the journal entry to show the sale of equipment is:

Cash	50,000	
Accumulated Depreciation	25,000	
Equipment		30,000
Gain on Sale		?

The $50,000 selling price was given. We know that the old equipment cost $30,000 because the company had to adjust the Equipment account by this amount to obtain the $470,000 ending account balance.

Analysis of the Accumulated Depreciation account provides the $25,000 adjustment to that account resulting from the sale. This account increased by the $40,000 depreciation expense. Therefore, it must have been reduced by $25,000 to provide the ending account balance.

In solving for the gain on sale, one approach is to set credits equal to debits. Since the debits total $75,000, the gain on sale must be $45,000 to provide for equality. Another way to look at the situation is to start with the book value of the equipment that was sold. The journal entry shows this to be $5,000 ($30,000 cost less $25,000 accumulated depreciation). Comparing this to the $50,000 selling price provides the $45,000 gain.

Selling price	$50,000
Book value	5,000
Gain on Sale	$45,000

The completed T-accounts are:

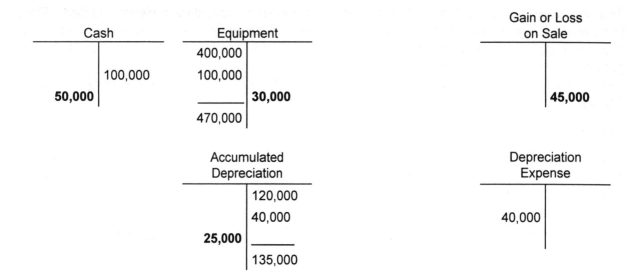

Cash	
	100,000
50,000	

Equipment	
400,000	
100,000	
_____	**30,000**
470,000	

Gain or Loss on Sale	
	45,000

Accumulated Depreciation	
	120,000
	40,000
25,000	_____
	135,000

Depreciation Expense	
40,000	

This is a fairly challenging problem. Congratulations if you're comfortable with it! If not, do the best you can with the other material in the book and ask your instructor to work similar problems in class.

Inventory and Cost of Goods Sold Exercises.

The Inventory, Accounts Payable, and Cost of Goods Sold accounts are closely related. First, companies purchase inventory on account. Then, they pay suppliers. Finally, the goods are sold. Inventory increases with purchases and decreases with the cost of goods sold. Accounts payable increase with purchases and decrease when suppliers are paid. The next several exercises develop analysis skills with respect to the Inventory, Accounts Payable, and Cost of Goods Sold accounts.

Exercise A5-7: Inventory and the Cost of Goods Sold. The Fry Company's cost of goods sold was $300,000. Using the beginning and ending account balances shown in the T-accounts, calculate the amount of inventory purchases.

Inventory		Accounts Payable		Cost of Goods Sold	
70,000			40,000		
50,000					

Solution

Given the $300,000 cost of goods sold, inventory purchases must have been $280,000 as shown in the following accounts:

Inventory		Accounts Payable		Cost of Goods Sold	
70,000			40,000		
280,000			**280,000**		
	300,000			**300,000**	
50,000					

The first step is to record the $300,000 cost of goods sold and reduction of inventory. Then, the addition to inventory must have been $280,000. Otherwise, ending inventory would not be $50,000.

The key is understanding that inventory increases with purchases and decreases when goods are sold. Try not to become upset if you have difficulty with this section. Work everything else thoroughly and ask your instructor to go over this material in class.

Exercise A5-8: Inventory and Accounts Payable. In this exercise the analyst works backward to calculate the cash paid for merchandise purchases. We know that the company first purchases inventory, then pays on account.

The Partridge Corporation's purchases were $700,000. Using the beginning and ending account balances shown in the Accounts Payable T-account, calculate the amount paid on account. Remember that accounts payable increase with purchases and decrease with cash payments.

Inventory		Cash		Accounts Payable	
25,000					40,000
					60,000

Solution

The amount paid on account was $680,000. Accounts payable increased by $700,000 when the company purchased inventory. Then, payables must have been reduced by $680,000 to result in the $60,000 ending balance. In most cases, reductions in payables mean payments.

Inventory		Cash		Accounts Payable	
25,000					40,000
700,000					**700,000**
		680,000	**680,000**		
					60,000

Exercise A5-9: Inventory, Accounts Payable, and the Cost of Goods Sold. The Bridge Corporation's cost of goods sold was $400,000. Beginning and ending Inventory and Accounts Payable balances are as shown. How much cash was paid for purchases?

Inventory	Cash	Accounts Payable	Cost of Goods Sold
80,000	600,000	10,000	
90,000		15,000	

Solution

The analysis of accounts shows that cash payments were $405,000. Your first step should be to reduce inventory for the cost of goods sold. Then, to explain the change in inventory, purchases must be $410,000.

We know that Accounts Payable was reduced with payments for inventory. Given the beginning and ending balances for this account and the $410,000 addition, payments must have been $405,000.

Inventory	Cash	Accounts Payable	Cost of Goods Sold
80,000	600,000	10,000	
410,000		**410,000**	
	405,000 **405,000**		
400,000			**400,000**
90,000		15,000	

Exercise A5-10: Inventory, Accounts Payable, and the Cost of Goods Sold. Beginning and ending Inventory and Accounts Payable balances are shown below in the T-accounts. The beginning cash balance is also shown. During the year, purchases were $100,000 and payments for these purchases were $95,000. Calculate the cost of goods sold and the ending cash balance.

Inventory	Cash	Accounts Payable	Cost of Goods Sold
30,000	100,000	20,000	
20,000		25,000	

Solution

The cost of goods sold is $110,000 and the ending cash balance is $5,000. As shown in the following T-accounts, inventory increases with purchases and decreases with the cost of goods sold. Similarly, payables increase with purchases on account and decrease with payments to suppliers.

Inventory		Cash		Accounts Payable		Cost of Goods Sold	
30,000		100,000			20,000		
100,000					**100,000**		
			95,000	95,000			
	110,000					**110,000**	
20,000		5,000			25,000		

The accounts show the $100,000 increase in inventory and accounts payable resulting from the purchases on account. The cost of goods sold has to be $110,000 to leave $20,000 as ending inventory.   Similarly, the beginning cash balance was reduced by the $95,000 payment on account. This leaves $5,000 as the ending cash balance.

The key to these exercises is knowing what items increase and decrease the account balances.

CHAPTER 6

TWENTY QUESTIONS

(Practice Exercises)

CHAPTER 6

TWENTY QUESTIONS
(Practice Exercises)

This chapter consists entirely of review exercises. Comfort with this material indicates a solid understanding of the accounting system and readiness to begin your classwork in accounting. It isn't necessary to work all practice exercises correctly on the first try. Review the appropriate chapters for missed material. Then, work these exercises as often as necessary.

The exercises are divided into two parts. Direct method exercises which emphasize the mechanics of the accounting system come first. Following this are indirect method problems which help develop skills in analysis and in estimating cash flows.

Exercise 6-1: Retained Earnings Warm-up. Three Sons, Incorporated began the year with retained earnings of $100,000. During the year, the corporation earned $40,000 and declared dividends of $15,000.

Changes in Retained Earnings

Beginning Retained Earnings	$100,000
Add: Income	_____
Less: Dividends Declared	_____
Ending Retained Earnings	_____

Three Sons should report ending retained earnings of:

a. $100,000
b.   115,000
c.   125,000
d.   140,000
e.   150,000

Solution. C.   Retained earnings increased by $25,000 to $125,000. We know that retained earnings increase with income ($40,000) and decrease with dividends ($15,000).

Changes in Retained Earnings

Beginning Retained Earnings	$100,000
Add: Income	40,000
Less: Dividends Declared	-15,000
Ending Retained Earnings	$125,000

Exercise 6-2: Balance Sheet Relationships. Portions of the Hot Asset Company's balance sheet were damaged when a nearby volcano erupted. Using your knowledge of balance sheet relationships, calculate the ending Capital Stock account balance.

Balance Sheet for the Hot Asset Company
At December 31, 19x8

Assets		Liabilities and Equity	
Cash	$40,000	Accounts Payable	$60,000
Inventory	100,000	Capital Stock	?
Investments	100,000	Retained Earnings	80,000
	$240,000		?

The balance in the Capital Stock account is:

a. $80,000
b. 100,000
c. 120,000
d. 150,000
e. 180,000

Solution. B. Given that Assets = Liabilities + Owners' Equity, liabilities and owners' equity must equal the $240,000 balance of the assets. This means that the balance in the Capital Stock account must be $100,000.

Balance Sheet for the Hot Assets Company
At December 31, 19x8

Assets		Liabilities and Equity	
Cash	$40,000	Accounts Payable	$60,000
Inventory	100,000	Capital Stock	100,000
Investments	100,000	Retained Earnings	80,000
	$240,000		$240,000

The next two exercises test your ability to classify balance sheet items as assets, liabilities, or owners' equity.

Exercise 6-3: Assets and Liabilities. All of the ButterCup Company's balance sheet accounts except cash are shown below:

ButterCup Company Balance Sheet Items
for the Year ended December 31, 19x1

Expenses Payable	$20,000
Retained Earnings	230,000
Inventory	10,000
Equipment	80,000
Capital Stock	110,000
Note Payable for Equipment	40,000
Factory	230,000

For this exercise, first classify the accounts as assets, liabilities, or owners' equity. Then, use the balance sheet equation to calculate the missing amounts.

ButterCup's cash balance is:

a. $40,000
b. 50,000
c. 70,000
d. 80,000
e. 100,000

Solution. D. The cash balance must be $80,000. Inventory, equipment, and the factory are assets. The remaining items reflect liabilities or owners' equity. Liabilities and owners' equity total $400,000. Therefore, since assets = liabilities + equity, assets must also total $40,000. The cash balance is the amount necessary to provide $400,000 in total assets. After substituting for cash, the completed balance sheet shows:

Balance Sheet for the ButterCup Company
At December 31, 19x1

Assets		Liabilities and Equity	
Cash	$80,000	Expenses Payable	$20,000
Inventory	10,000	Note Payable	40,000
Equipment	80,000	Capital Stock	110,000
Factory	230,000	Retained Earnings	230,000
	$400,000		$400,000

Exercise 6-4: Classifying Accounts. This exercise involves recognition of asset, liability, and owners' equity accounts.

The Wishy Company's balance sheet at the beginning of 19x6 shows the following:

Accounts	Amounts
Cash	$500
Capital Stock	100
Accounts Receivable	48
Accumulated Depreciation	90
Accounts Payable	30
Inventory	10
Retained Earnings	528
Equipment	190

Wishy's assets (net of accumulated depreciation) on January 1, 19x6 total:

a. $621
b. 658
c. 660
d. 710
e. 719

Solution. B. Wishy's total assets on January 1 are $658. The assets are cash, accounts receivable, inventory, and equipment. Accumulated Depreciation, a contra account, reduces the balance of total assets. All remaining accounts are liability or equity accounts. This is seen in the following complete balance sheet.

Balance Sheet for the Wishy Company
at January 1, 19x6

Assets		Liabilities and Equity	
Cash	$500	Accounts Payable	$30
Accounts Receivable	48	Capital Stock	100
Inventory	10	Retained Earnings	528
Equipment	190		$658
Accumulated Depreciation	-90		
	$658		

Exercise 6-5: Transactions. The Wishy Company examined in the previous exercise begins 19x6 with the following balance sheet:

Balance Sheet for the Wishy Company
at January 1, 19x6

Assets		Liabilities and Equity	
Cash	$500	Accounts Payable	$30
Accounts Receivable	48	Capital Stock	100
Inventory	10	Retained Earnings	528
Equipment	190		$658
Accumulated Depreciation	-90		
	$658		

This exercise involves recording transactions and adjusting entries. The challenge is to find the end-of-year total assets. It is not necessary to close the books for this determination.

1.	Shareholders contribute cash to the business	$40
2.	The business buys inventory on account	610
3.	Sales on account	900
4.	Collections of receivables	880
5.	Payments on account	620
6.	Salary expense (payments $90)	100
7.	Declared dividends to shareholders (paid $25)	30

At the end of the year, Wishy uses the following information to make adjusting entries:

a.	Depreciation expense	$40
b.	Ending inventory	25

T-accounts are provided to help organize your work.

Cash		Accounts Payable		Capital Stock		Retained Earnings	
500			30		100		528

Accounts Receivable		Dividends Payable		Dividends Declared		Sales Revenue	
48							

Inventory		Salaries Payable				Cost of Goods Sold	
10							

Equipment						Salaries	
190							

Accumulated Depreciation						Depreciation Expense	
	90						

Wishy's assets (net of accumulated depreciation) on December 31, 19x6 total:

a. $742
b.   758
c.   823
d.   827
e.   838

Solution. E. The ending total assets sum to $838. Wishy's completed T-accounts and journal entries follow:

Cash		Accounts Payable		Capital Stock		Retained Earnings	
500			30		100		528
40			**610**		**40**		
880	620	620	___		140		
	90		20				
	25						
___							
685							

Accounts Receivable		Dividends Payable		Dividends Declared		Sales Revenue	
48			5	30			900
900	880						
68							

Inventory		Salaries Payable				Cost of Goods Sold	
10			10			595	
610	595						
25							

Equipment				Salaries	
190				**100**	

Accumulated Depreciation				Depreciation Expense	
	90			**40**	
	40				
	130				

The journal entries are:

1. **Shareholders contribute cash**

Cash	40	
Capital Stock		40

2. **The business buys inventory on account**

Inventory	610	
Accounts Payable		610

3. **Sales on account**

Accounts Receivable	900	
Sales		900

4. **Collections of receivables**

Cash	880	
Accounts Receivable		880

5. **Payments on account**

Accounts Payable	620	
Cash		620

6. **Salary expense $100 (payments $90)**

Salary Expense	100	
Cash		90
Salaries Payable		10

7. **Declared $30 dividends to shareholders (paid $25)**

Dividends Declared	30	
Cash		25
Dividends Payable		5

a. **Depreciation expense $40**

Depreciation Expense	40	
Accumulated Depreciation		40

b. **Ending inventory $25 ($595 sold)**

Cost of Goods Sold	595	
Inventory		595

Exercise 6-6: Closing the Books. Now, it's time for the Wishy Company to close the books and determine ending retained earnings. Before closing, the account balances are:

Cash	Accounts Payable	Capital Stock	Retained Earnings
685	20	140	528

Accounts Receivable	Dividends Payable	Dividends Declared	Sales Revenue
68	5	30	900

Inventory	Salaries Payable		Cost of Goods Sold
25	10		595

Equipment			Salaries
190			100

Accumulated Depreciation		Income Summary	Depreciation Expense
130			40

The ending retained earnings balance is:

a. $612
b.   624
c.   637
d.   663
e.   704

Solution. D. Ending retained earnings are $663. Steps in the closing process are shown in the following T-accounts.

Cash		Accounts Payable		Capital Stock		Retained Earnings	
685			20		140		528
							165
						30	____
							663

Accounts Receivable		Dividends Payable		Dividends Declared		Sales Revenue	
68			5	30			900
					30	**900**	

Inventory		Salaries Payable			Cost of Goods Sold	
25			10		595	
						595

Equipment				Salaries	
190				100	
					100

Accumulated Depreciation		**Income Summary**		Depreciation Expense	
	130		900	40	
		595			**40**
		100			
		40	____		
			165		
		165			

You could find retained earnings in this exercise without the closing entries. From the previous exercise, the assets are $838 and liabilities total $35. Thus, owners' equity is $803. Since we know that capital stock is $140, retained earnings must be $663.

Please refer to Chapters 2, 3, and 4 for help with these concepts.

Exercise 6-7: Interest Receivable. The Interest Receivable account increases with interest income and decreases as payments are received.

At the beginning of the year, the Ruckus Corporation's Interest Receivable account balance is $9,000. During the year, the company earned $100,000 in interest and collected $102,000. T-accounts are provided to help you find the ending Interest Receivable account balance.

Cash	Interest Receivable	Interest Revenue
	9,000	

The ending Interest Receivable account balance is:

a. $5,000
b.   7,000
c.   9,000
d. 11,000
e. 13,000

Solution. B. The ending receivable is $7,000. First we increase the interest receivable by $100,000 to reflect revenue. Then, we reduce the receivable by $102,000, the amount collected.

Cash	Interest Receivable	Interest Revenue
	9,000	
	100,000	100,000
102,000	___ | 102,000	
	7,000	

Exercise 6-8: Prepaid Accounts. Prepaid accounts increase with payments. They decrease with expenses.

The Sneeze Corporation begins the year with $2,000 in prepaid insurance. During the year, Sneeze pays $21,000 for insurance. Insurance expense during the year is $22,000. Sneeze's relevant T-accounts are:

The ending Prepaid Insurance account balance is:

a. $1,000
b.   2,000
c.   3,000
d.   4,000
e.   5,000

Solution. A. The ending Prepaid Insurance account balance is $1,000. This account increases by the $21,000 payment and decreases by the $22,000 expense as shown in the following entries.

Exercise 6-9: Accounting for Depreciable Property. The Fever Group buys new recording equipment for $60,000. The group expects to use the equipment for four years and then sell it for $20,000.

At the end of <u>two</u> years, the Accumulated Depreciation account balance will be:

a. $0
b.   10,000
c.   15,000
d.   20,000
e.   23,000

Solution. D. Accumulated depreciation will be $20,000 at the end of two years. The annual depreciation is:

$$\text{Annual depreciation expense} = \text{Amount to be depreciated} / \text{Expected life}$$

$$= (\text{Cost-Residual value}) / \text{Expected life}$$

$$= (\$60,000 - \$20,000) / 4 \text{ years} = \$10,000 \text{ per year}$$

After two years, accumulated depreciation will be $20,000.

Review Chapter 5 for help with plant and equipment accounts.

Exercise 6-10: Accounting for Depreciable Property. The Fever Group bought new recording equipment for $60,000 and expected to use the equipment for four years and then sell it for $20,000. Previously, we determined that depreciation is $10,000 per year. At the end of <u>three</u> years, Fever actually sells the equipment for $5,000. Complete the T-accounts just prior to sale:

```
                                    Accumulated
         Equipment                  Depreciation
      _____     _____
        60,000 |                            |
               |                            |
               |                            |
               |                            |
               |                            |
```

Then find the gain or loss on sale.

Selling price	_____
Book value	_____
Loss on Sale	_____

Finally, record the journal entry to be sure you have a loss rather than a gain.

Cash	_____	
Accumulated Depreciation	_____	
Loss on Sale	_____	
Equipment		_____

The gain or loss on sale is:

a. $25,000 loss
b.   10,000 loss
c.   none
d.   10,000 gain
e.   25,000 gain

Solution. A. Fever will report a $25,000 loss. At the end of three years, accumulated depreciation is $30,000 ($10,000 per year). Subtracting this amount from the $60,000 cost results in a $30,000 book value. Since the selling price is only $5,000, the loss is $25,000. Just prior to sale, the T-accounts show:

Equipment		Accumulated Depreciation	
60,000			10,000
			10,000
			10,000
			30,000

Comparison of the selling price and book value shows:

Selling price	$5,000
Less: Book value	-30,000
Loss on Sale	$25,000

The journal entry to record the sale is:

Cash	5,000	
Accumulated Depreciation	30,000	
Loss on Sale	25,000	
Equipment		60,000

APPENDIX TO CHAPTER 6– EXERCISES IN FINANCIAL ANALYSIS

Exercise A6-1: Retained Earnings. The Three Daughters Corporation began the year with $200,000 of retained earnings. During the year, the corporation earned $60,000. Ending retained earnings are $220,000.

Changes in Retained Earnings

Beginning Retained Earnings	$200,000
Add: Income	_____
Less: Dividends Declared	_____
Ending Retained Earnings	$220,000

Three Daughters declared the following dividends to Sandra, Sally, and Susie, the three shareholders:

a. $20,000
b. 40,000
c. 60,000
d. 80,000
e. 90,000

Solution. B. Retained earnings increased by $20,000. Since income was $60,000, dividends must have been $40,000.

Changes in Retained Earnings

Beginning Retained Earnings	$200,000
Add: Income	60,000
Less: Dividends Declared	-40,000
Ending Retained Earnings	$220,000

Exercise A6-2: Retained Earnings. The Westin Brothers Corporation begins the year with retained earnings of $300,000. During the year, the company reports income. It then declares dividends of $30,000. Ending retained earnings are $310,000.

Changes in Retained Earnings

Beginning Retained Earnings	$300,000
Add: Income	_____
Less: Dividends Declared	_____
Ending Retained Earnings	_____

The Westin Brothers' income is for the year is:

a. $10,000
b.   25,000
c.   30,000
d.   40,000
e.   50,000

Solution. D. Retained earnings increased by $10,000. Dividends reduced retained earnings by $30,000. Therefore, income must have been $40,000.

Changes in Retained Earnings

Beginning Retained Earnings	$300,000
Add: Income	40,000
Less: Dividends Declared	-30,000
Ending Retained Earnings	$310,000

Exercise A6-3: Retained Earnings. The Fruitcake Corporation begins the year with retained earnings of $500,000. During the year, the company produces more fruitcakes than it can sell and reports a loss. Fruitcake then declares dividends of $20,000. Ending retained earnings are $470,000.

Changes in Retained Earnings

Beginning Retained Earnings	$500,000
Less: Loss	_____
Less: Dividends Declared	_____
Ending Retained Earnings	_____

The loss reported by the Fruitcake Corporation for the year is:

a. $5,000
b.   7,000
c.   9,000
d. 10,000
e. 15,000

Solution. D. The loss was $10,000. Since dividends reduced retained earnings by $20,000, the loss had to be $10,000 in order for retained earnings to fall by $30,000.

Changes in Retained Earnings

Beginning Retained Earnings	$500,000
Less: Loss	-10,000
Dividends Declared	-20,000
Ending Retained Earnings	$470,000

Exercise A6-4: Basic Asset, Liability, Equity Relationships. The Fast Break Corporation began business in early 19x4. Investors paid $60,000 for shares of capital stock early in the year. No additional shares were issued during the year. At the end of the year, net assets (assets less liabilities) are $90,000. Dividends of $20,000 were declared and paid during 19x4. (Hint: Except for the initial investment, capital stock did not change during the year. If we know the ending net assets and capital stock, we can calculate ending retained earnings.)

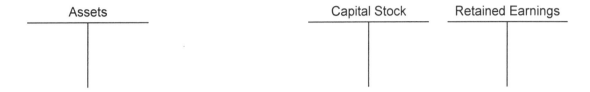

Income for 19x4 is:

a. $5,000
b. 20,000
c. 30,000
d. 40,000
e. 50,000

Solution. E. Owners' equity (net assets) is given as $90,000 at the end of the year. We know that owners' equity has two main components, capital stock and retained earnings. Since capital stock is $60,000, retained earnings must be $30,000. We also know that dividends were $20,000. This means that retained earnings first increased by $50,000; then decreased by $20,000 to end at $30,000 after dividends. The $50,000 increase is income. This is shown in the following accounts:

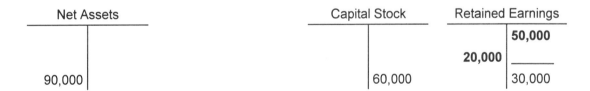

The key to this exercise is understanding that owners' equity consists of capital stock and retained earnings. Generally, capital stock changes only when the company receives additional funds from investors in exchange for shares. Except in unusual circumstances, retained earnings change only as a result of income (or loss) and dividends.

Exercise A6-5: Basic Asset, Liability, Equity Relationships with Losses. Pancake Villa, a breakfast restaurant, decided to extend its hours and serve pancakes all day until about 10 p.m. Unfortunately, the restaurant only serves breakfast food and the afternoon and evening business is extremely slow. At the beginning of the year, capital stock was $100,000 and retained earnings were $20,000. The business did not have any liabilities. Ending assets were $128,000. During the year, shareholders invested an additional $25,000 in capital stock. Dividends declared during the year were $10,000.

Assets	Capital Stock	Retained Earnings
	100,000	20,000

Pancake Villa's loss for the year is:

a. $5,000
b.   6,000
c.   7,000
d.   8,000
e.   10,000

Solution. C. The loss was $7,000. First, calculate the ending Capital Stock account balance ($100,000 plus $25,000) Then, with ending assets given as $128,000, we know that ending retained earnings are only $3,000. How could retained earnings fall to only $3,000? The beginning balance was $20,000. Dividends reduced this to $10,000. Then, a loss must have caused the additional reduction to $3,000. This is shown as follows:

Assets		Capital Stock	Retained Earnings
120,000		100,000	20,000
25,000		25,000	
	10,000		10,000
	7,000		7,000
128,000		125,000	3,000

Please refer to Chapter 1 for more practice with these concepts.

Exercise A6-6: Interest Receivable. The Mallard Corporation began the year with $8,000 of interest receivable and ended the year with interest receivable of $5,000. During the year the company earned $80,000 of interest revenue.

The cash collected from borrowers was:

a. $77,000
b. 79,000
c. 80,000
d. 81,000
e. 83,000

Solution. E. The cash collections were $83,000. First, record the $80,000 revenue and increase in receivables. Collections had to be $83,000 to provide the $5,000 ending cash balance.

Review Chapter 4 for help with receivables and payables.

Exercise A6-7: Prepaid Accounts. The Flag Corporation begins the year with $12,000 in prepaid rent and ends the year with $15,000 of prepaid rent. During the year, rent expense is $200,000. The relevant T-accounts are:

The amount paid to the landlord during the year was:

a. $197,000
b.   199,000
c.   200,000
d.   201,000
e.   203,000

Solution. E. Flag Corporation paid the landlord $203,000. The $200,000 rent expense reduces prepaid rent. Therefore, prepaid rent must be increased by $203,000 to provide the $15,000 ending balance.   Prepaid rent increases when cash is paid to the landlord. The transactions are shown in the following T-accounts:

Prepaid accounts were covered in Chapter 5.

Exercise A6-8: Plant and Equipment Accounts. At the beginning of the year, the Street Company's account balances for Equipment and Accumulated Depreciation were $300,000 and $100,000 respectively. By year end, the balances had increased to $400,000 and $151,000. Depreciation expense for the year was $70,000. The company paid $150,000 for new equipment and sold old equipment at a $25,000 loss. Your mission is to determine the selling price of the old equipment.

Equipment	Accumulated Depreciation	Cash	Depreciation Expense
300,000	100,000		
400,000	151,000		

Loss on Sale

To record the sale:

Cash	_____
Accumulated Depreciation	_____
Loss on Sale	_____
Equipment	_____

The old equipment's selling price is:

a. $2,000
b. 4,000
c. 6,000
d. 8,000
e. 10,000

Solution. C. The selling price is $6,000. Just prior to the sale, after entering depreciation expense and the purchase of new equipment, the relevant accounts appear as follows:

Equipment		Accumulated Depreciation		Cash		Depreciation Expense	
300,000			100,000				
150,000				**150,000**			
_____			**70,000**			**70,000**	
400,000			151,000				

Loss on Sale
_____

The journal entry to record the sale is:

Cash	6,000	
Accumulated Depreciation	19,000	
Loss on Sale	25,000	
Equipment		50,000

Both the equipment and accumulated depreciation balances can be determined from our knowledge of factors that cause changes in these accounts. The cost of equipment sold had to be $50,000 since this is the most straightforward explanation of the change in the Equipment account balance. Similarly, accumulated depreciation on the item sold had to be $19,000 to explain ending accumulated depreciation. This means that the book value of the items sold was $31,000.

Since the loss on sale is given, the cash received must have been $6,000. Now that we know the amount, we can confirm that $6,000 was received.

Selling price	$6,000
Less: Book value	-31,000
Loss on Sale	$25,000

Exercise A6-9: Inventory, Accounts Payable, and the Cost of Goods Sold. The beginning and ending balances for the Inventory account were $20,000 and $24,000. For accounts payable, the beginning and ending account balances were $5,000 and $4,000. During the year, the cost of goods sold was $100,000. We know that inventory increases with purchases and decreases with the cost of goods sold. Accounts payable also increase with purchases. Payments reduce accounts payable.

Inventory	Cash	Accounts Payable	Cost of Goods Sold
20,000	600,000	5,000	
24,000		4,000	

The cash paid for inventory was:

a. $96,000
b. 100,000
c. 101,000
d. 104,000
e. 105,000

Solution. E. The cash paid for inventory was $105,000. We know that the cost of goods sold reduced inventory by $100,000. This means that the company purchased inventory for $104,000. Otherwise, the ending Inventory account balance would not be the amount shown. Since inventory purchases were $104,000, accounts payable must have also increased by this amount. Then, payments had to be $105,000 to result in the $4,000 ending amount for Accounts Payable.

Inventory		Cash		Accounts Payable		Cost of Goods Sold	
20,000	100,000	600,000			5,000	100,000	
104,000					104,000		
			105,000	105,000			
24,000					4,000		

Inventory, accounts payable, and cost of goods sold relationships were covered in Chapter 5.

Exercise A6-10: Dividends Payable. During the year, the Butch Company declared $30,000 in dividends. Beginning and ending Dividend Payable account balances were $5,000 and $5,500. Remember that the Dividends Payable account increases when dividends are declared. The account decreases when dividends are paid.

Cash	Dividends Payable	Dividends Declared
	5,000	
	―――	
	5,500	

The dividend payments (cash) during the year were:

a. $28,000
b.   28,500
c.   29,000
d.   29,500
e.   30,000

Solution. D. Dividend payments were $29,500. Dividends payable increase by the amount of dividends declared and decrease with cash payments. The Butch Company's dividends declared were $30,000 and the payable increased by $500. This means that payments were only $29,500. The following T-accounts show the dividend declaration and payment as a compound entry:

Cash	Dividends Payable	Dividends Declared
	5,000	
29,500	**500**	**30,000**
	5,500	

Solving for cash using two single entries leads to the same conclusion.

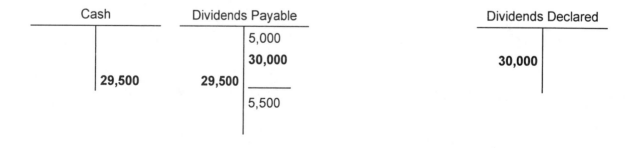